The
YARNS
of
BILLY
BORKER

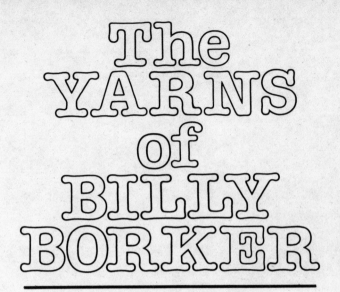

The YARNS of BILLY BORKER

by Frank Hardy

illustrated by VANE

introduced by CLEMENT SEMMLER

ANGUS & ROBERTSON PUBLISHERS

ANGUS & ROBERTSON PUBLISHERS
London • Sydney • Melbourne • Singapore • Manila

First published 1965
A&R Modern Comedies edition first published by
Angus & Robertson Publishers, Australia, 1977
This Arkon paperback edition 1980

© Frank Hardy 1965

National Library of Australia
card number and ISBN 0 207 13442 1

Printed in Australia by Hedges & Bell Pty Ltd

Preface

When the Billy Borker series appeared on ABC Television critics and viewers alike hailed it as one of the few original and authentic contributions to Australian television yet.

For Frank Hardy has achieved something as significant as it is considerable—he has created Billy Borker as someone who "sees something immortal in the ordinary people". Truthful Jones, Timetable Tommy, Sheckles Mitchell, Dooley Franks from Parramatta (hero of "The Great Australian Larrikin", likely I am sure to pass into Australian folk-story), Greenfingers Stratton (who "could grow orchids in a concrete footpath"), Hungry Hanrahan, the taxi driver ("the greatest pot-sitter, multiple loader and fare-fleecer that ever sat behind a steering wheel")—these and a dozen more make the tradition of mateship and the common folk; they are bloodbrothers to Hardy's Benson Valley characters, By-the-Way Lawton, Matches Anderson, Turns-Around Atkins and the rest. From the Earl of Zetland Hotel in Adelaide to the Globe Hotel in Brisbane, Borker has spun his whoppers; the material of his stories ranges from the wharves of Wellington to the goldfields of Kalgoorlie.

Borker's philosophy, which is Hardy's of course, stems from the ordinary pleasures and problems of ordinary people: beer ("the gargle has ruined many a good man"); money (whether you "can get in front or not"); and the horses. Here Borker is in his element, and some of Hardy's turf stories are as amusing and colloquially told as any in Australian literature since Banjo Paterson's "The Oracle". "It's not a sport, mate," says Borker, "it's a lottery with four-legged tickets," and proceeds to spin out the saga of Black Snowy and Integrity Hanson in "There's No Certainties in Racing" ("unless you could buy the Sunday papers on Saturday morning"). As for "Everyone Reads the Signs They Want to See"—the story of Murphy the Bookmaker and his faithful friends Ticktacker Tom and Ron the Runner—keep this one till last, and you'll still be laughing at the end of the day. It's in the Runyon class.

Shot through this collection is Frank Hardy's particular brand of laconic irony which brings out the humour in adversity, but with a built-in iconoclasm that sends up a few of our conventions and institutions too. There's no more thieving goes on at the wharves in Woolloomooloo than in the Stock Exchange, is one of Borker's pet sayings; and he tells in one of his stories of the "Yank" who had never heard of Sydney until Australia was mentioned: "Ah yeah, that's where we sell all our old films to the television stations."

Billy Borker, of the people, yet larger than life, is thus of the stuff of legend; he is in the same bracket as Paterson's Saltbush Bill and John Manifold's Bogong Jack. Like every dinkum Aussie who survives in our folk history his epitaph will rest in the words of Ian Mudie's poem "They'll Tell You About Me" ("Me, I'm the man that dug the Murray for Sturt to sail down . . .")

> if you'd like to know more of me
> inquire at the pub at Tennant Creek

or at any drover's camp
or shearing shed
or shout any bloke in any bar a drink
or yarn to any bloke asleep on any beach
they'll tell you all about me
they'll tell you more than I know myself.

CLEMENT SEMMLER

Contents

Illustrations

Illustrations

I

The Only Fair Dinkum Raffle Ever Run in Australia

(as told by Billy Borker in Millers Oceanic Hotel, Coogee)

D ID I ever tell you about the only fair dinkum raffle ever run in Australia?

No, I don't think you did. Have another drink and tell me about it.

Don't mind if I do. It happened during the Depression years. Things was crook with me at the time and I was no Robinson Crusoe, I can tell you. Funny thing about a depression. The silvertails always say the unemployed don't want work; then comes a war and there's no more unemployed. Now where do them unemployed get to? Get killed in the war, I s'pose.

You could be right at that—but get on with your story. Actually, you said before you'd tell me about an old age pensioner who—what did he do again?

Cleaned up three policemen during the shearers' strike. But first I must tell you about the only fair dinkum raffle ever run in Australia. You never want to buy a raffle ticket. It's a bad habit to get into, like paying your income tax and backing racehorses; once you start, you can't stop. I've run a few raffles in my time, and I know what I'm talking about.

Oh, I don't know. A lot of honest raffles run, I reckon.

Well, every man's entitled to his own opinion but opinions are funny things: a man who gets wrong opinions either ends up in jail or in Parliament.

You'd better tell me about that raffle. . . . What was it again?

The only fair dinkum raffle ever run in Australia. I ran it meself, so I ought to know. . . .

How did it come to happen?

Well, it was during the Depression like I said and there was a bloke next door to me who kept chooks. Out at Woolloomooloo, it was. I used to keep looking over the fence at them fowls, clucking and pecking away, and I used to say to meself: "Them chooks are eating their heads off in there while human beings are starving. It isn't right. Them chooks ought to be raffled." I said it to Clara-girl: "Them chooks ought to be raffled."

Who's Clara-girl?

My wife, Clara. A fine woman—in her place, but she ain't there yet. But I'll say this for her: she did agree that them chooks should be raffled. So, one night, I dived over the fence and grabbed two big black chooks. Orphingtons, they were. You wouldn't credit the noise a chook can make when it knows it's going to be raffled! Fit to wake their owner up. At last, I got hold of 'em and put 'em in a bag under the bed.

And what has stealing two chooks got to do with a fair dinkum raffle?

Comin' to that—not a bad drop of beer this—well, next day was Saturday and I went down to the pub. And I've got these two chooks in a spud bag with their

14

"I pinched the two chooks . . . !"

heads stickin' out two holes. Threepence a ticket—threepence was a lot of dough in those days. Well, I sold a book of tickets and, just to show it was a fair dinkum raffle, I asked the publican to draw it. . . .

But how could the raffle be fair dinkum?

My father wouldn't have worn you for a bet. You keep interrupting and ruining the story.

Sorry. Have another drink.

Well, anyway, a fella named Smith won the chooks. A little fella with sandy hair and a white-handled pocket-knife. So I gave him the two chooks, bags and all. Think he'd won the lottery. The only fair dinkum raffle ever run. . . .

But what about your next door neighbour? You stole his chooks. It wasn't such a fair dinkum raffle.

Coming to that. I had a guilty conscience about stealing them chooks; so I followed this fella Smith home. It was getting dark. He goes in and tells his missus about the chooks, then puts 'em out in the wood-shed. I'm hanging round the front gate and watching and listening in the night. Went home and had me tea; fried bread and tomatoes. The only fair dinkum raffle ever run in Australia.

But what about the bloke you stole the two chooks from?

Well, you see, it was this way. I was worried about him, so that same night, I went back to this here Smith bloke's place, and pinched the two chooks out of the shed.

And gave them back to the original owner?

That's for sure. The only fair dinkum raffle. . . .

Just a minute. That fella Smith who won the raffle. He paid for his ticket—threepence.

That's right. Well, I thought of that. So after I returned the chooks to their owner I went back to Smith's place and pushed a thrupenny bit under his front door. . . . It was like I told you—the only fair dinkum raffle ever run in Australia.

You win. I must admit you tell a good story.

Ah, they're really my father's stories. That reminds me, did I ever tell you about the crookest raffle ever run in Australia?

I've got to go now. You can tell me tomorrow.

Won't be here tomorrow. I'll be raffling a couple of chickens in a pub out at Redfern.

2

The Violinist from Chinkapook

(as told by Billy Borker in the
Golden Fleece Hotel, Melbourne)

D ID I ever tell you about the violinist from Chinkapook who ran all the way up to the forward
line bouncing the ball?

No, I don't think you did. Have another beer and
tell me about it. By the way, where do you get all these
stories? Do you make them up?

Oh, no. They're all true. They're not my stories at
all, they're really my father's stories.

Your father was a story writer, was he?

Not him! He was a can-washer in a milk factory—
been a shearer before that. He was a good story teller,
though. But, like all the best story tellers, he didn't
write his stories down. That's why I tell his stories—so's
people will get to know them. Stories you read in books
and newspapers are no good; they're made up about
murderers, thieves, businessmen, gold-diggers, rich men's
wives with tight sweaters and no children; about cow-
boys, gangsters, and newspaper reporters. Not worth
reading.

I'm a story writer myself, as a matter of fact.

No offence meant.

It's all right. Tell me about the violinist from Chinka-pook. What did he do again?

He ran all the way up to the forward line, bouncing the ball. Lanky fella, he was, with long skinny legs like bent flagpoles. Worst footballer in the district, but a real good kick. Best kick who ever played. Could kick a ball a hundred yards, standing. Better kick than Dave McNamara. Trouble was he couldn't get the ball to kick it. Biggest squib that ever played, but keen. Played a few games in the local team, but never got a kick, so they dropped him out.

I suppose he gave the game up?

Not him. Kept comin' to practice Tuesdays and Thursdays, regular as the post-office clock. You know how it is. He was a very good violinist, but his ambition was to become a league footballer. That's the way people are—always wanting to be someone else. Well, one day, the captain of the Chinkapook Football Club got a brainwave. Said to the selection committee, give this bloke another trial, put him in the goals. Full-back. He'll kick off to the centre every time the other team scores a behind. Selection committee put him in as full-back. Most remarkable game I ever saw. That's what my father said, "Most remarkable game I ever saw!"

I suppose this bloke played a good game, kicking off to the centre and so on?

Never touched the ball till the last quarter. The other team—Ouyen, I think it was—kicked sixteen goals straight without a behind. The most remarkable game . . .

You said that before. Have another drink and get on with the story.

Well, Ouyen kicked sixteen goals and Chinkapook

"He grabs the ball and runs for his life . . . !"

fourteen goals, seven behinds. Needed a goal to win with a few minutes to go. Windy day—all the play on one side of the ground—all the players on one side of the ground, too, needless to say. Well, this lanky bloke is standing on his own in the goals, see. Someone kicks the ball and it hits him in the face, and wakes him up. He grabs it and runs for his life round the wing, where there's no players, his legs flaying like a windmill in a high wind. Bouncing the ball every few yards, he was. Frightened as a sparrow locked in a barn.

Did the players in the other team run across and stop him?

No fear, his team mates shepherded them off. Well, he ran like a cartwheel without a rim, right up to the forward line, about sixty yards out. Easy for him from there—being able to kick better than Dave McNamara, as I said.

I suppose he kicked a goal and won the game?

No such luck. He was just going to kick one of his mighty punts on the run when the final bell rang. He never got another game after that.

So he went back to playing the violin again?

Matter of fact, last I heard of him he had sold his fiddle, and was selling place cards on commission for a barber in Mildura.

3

Not Like Here in Woolloomooloo

(as told by Billy Borker in
Mallett's Inn, Sydney)

D ID I ever tell you about the fella from Woolloomooloo whose life's ambition was to go to Paris?

No, I don't think you did. Have a drink and
tell me about him.

Thanks. Well, this fella used to be always saying
he'd like to go to Paris, see. Said it in the pub. Said
it nearly every day at smoko. Wharfie, he was. Couldn't
afford a trip on the Manly ferry—but wanted to go t.
Paris.

Oh, I don't know—here's your beer—wharfies don't
make bad money.

Twenty-five quid a week and half the cargo, some
mugs reckon. Don't you believe it. But there's no money
to be made on the waterfront these days—except appear-
ance money. I know what I'm talking about, brother.
Worked on the wharf for years, meself. There's no
more thieving goes on there than on the Stock Exchange,
I can tell you. Anyway, this bloke kept saying he
wanted to go to Paris. Used to stand in the pub at
Woolloomooloo with his mates of a Saturday morning,
spending his last dollar on beer and saying he wanted
to go to Paris. Funny thing that, isn't it? People always

want to be somewhere else, to do things they can't do. . . .

I think I've heard you say that before. Did this fella get to Paris?

There you go again. Trying to make me get ahead of my story. My father always said. . . .

I know what he always said. Get on with your story.

Well, as I was saying before you so rudely interrupted, people are always wanting to be someone else. I've heard Bob Menzies would like to be a whisky taster at the Royal Show.

You don't tell. . . .

So help me. A bloke told me that in a pub at Kalgoorlie. . . . Anyway, this fella from Woolloomooloo kept saying he'd like to go to Paris. Even said it to his wife in bed one night. She took a jagged view of his ambition, as you can understand, a woman will trust a man anywhere except in Paris—that didn't stop him wanting to go. As it turned out his wife died after ptomaine poisoning from drinking you-know-who's beer. And being a widower increased his ambition to go to Paris. . . .

Aw, come on! Did he go or not?

Coming to that. It turned out that one Saturday morning his mates were standing in the pub at Woolloomooloo when he rushed in and said he'd won the lottery. Shouted for the bar to prove it. Well, needless to say, his mates gave him plenty of advice. You can always get advice on how to spend money but never how to earn it. . . .

Did he go to Paris or not? Here, have another drink.

Just to be sociable. One bloke suggested he should send his kids to the university. "What," he answered. "And turn them into toffs and scabs? Not on your bloody life." "Buy yourself a house," another fella urged. "The old house I'm living in has done me for twenty years," he told him. "Well, buy a big Yankee car," someone else advised. "Can't drive a car," he said. "Well, buy a pushbike," another of his mates suggested. "Haven't got a peddler's licence," he replied. "It's no good arguing with me. I'm going to Paris. And I'm not coming back until all the money's gone." Within a week, he jobbed the panno, snatched his time and bought an air ticket to gay Paree.

Here's your beer. How did he get on?

Thanks. Matter of fact nothing more was heard of him. . . .

Well, that's a poor sort of a story, that is. No point to it.

Give me time; give me time. My father always said . . .

Aw, to hell with your father. Did he come back or not?

What goes up must come down. His mates often wondered what became of him. I was about to say that he was never heard of again—until one Saturday his mates arrived at the pub as usual, and there he was, large as life, standing in the corner all dressed up to go on afternoon shift, spending his last dollar on beer.

Spent the lot, had he?

A course he had. No good ever came of a working man winning the lottery. Well, his mates crowded around him. And asked a lot of questions—about Paris, needless to say. They asked more questions than Bob Dyer. "What was the weather like in Paris?" "Not like here in Woolloomooloo. It was beautiful. I was there for six months in the spring and summer and the sun

24

shining every day. Not too hot, not too cold. Not like here in Woolloomooloo where it's either too hot or too cold, either raining cats and dogs or a drought. Not like here in Woolloomooloo, I can tell you." "And what was the tucker like in Paris?" another fellow queried. "The tucker was beautiful," he told them. "Not like here in Woolloomooloo. You sit on the foot-path and have your meals and watch the crowds go by while you sip your coffee. And the food? Delicious! Not cooked too much; not too underdone. Turtle soup, steak, and beautiful cheese—not like the bunghole here in Woolloomooloo—and frog's legs done in beautiful sauce. They use seasoning in the sauce that would make the sole of a leper's boot taste like a filet mignon. Boy, that was tucker. Not like the pies and sausages you get at the hamburger joints and Greek cafés here in Woolloomooloo. And glorious wine, the nectar of the gods! And German beer! Not like the watered-down grog you get here in Woolloomooloo."

You make me feel thirsty. Have another beer.

Don't mind if I do. Mightn't be as good as in Paris, but I'll force it down.

This story better have a good ending.

All my father's stories have good endings. Well, they kept asking him about Paris. "Did you go to one of them there night clubs, where the women dance in the nude?" another mate asked. "I went to the Folies Bergère every night." "And what was it like?" "Not like these crummy floor shows here in Woolloomooloo, I can tell you. It was terrific. Music. Champagne. Floor show. Dancing girls, with nothing on, not a stitch. Not like here in Woolloomooloo."

I still can't see any point in this story. . . .

Barley Charley—give me time to finish. Another bloke says to him: "And what were those French women like?" "Ah, not like these bags here in Woolloomooloo who are either too fat or too thin, too tall or too short. And mutton done up as lamb, most of them. These French women are glorious—not too fat, not too thin, not too tall, not too short. Beautiful clothes and perfect figures. An old French bag is better looking than a teenage model here in Woolloomooloo."

Here's your beer. He was real wrapped up in Paris, all right.

You can say that again. And they asked him plenty of questions—like a bosses' lawyer in the Arbitration Court. "They'd treat you well, those French women, I s'pose," another fella said. "Would they ever. Champagne and a chicken dinner chucked in." He got his money's worth in Paris, by the sound of him—"not like here in Woolloomooloo."

There's no end to this story by the sound of it.

All good things come to an end—like this bloke's trip to Paris. At last one fella asked him: "Did you ever kiss a French woman?" "My bloody oath, I did," he replied. "And what was it like?" Well, that rocked him a bit. He looked this way and that, drained his last beer and said: "Oh, just like here in Woolloomooloo, come to think of it. Just like here in Woolloomooloo."

Yes, not bad. Real good, as a matter of fact. It grows on you, that story. A beauty. Have another drink on the strength of it.

Not now. I've just got time to catch the lottery office before it closes. Think I'll buy a few tickets. Wouldn't mind a trip to Paris meself.

26

4

The Mosquitoes are Big in the Territory

(as told by Billy Borker in the
New York Hotel, Pyrmont)

Dᴵᴰ I ever tell you about the old aged pensioner who cleaned up three policemen during the shearers' strike?

No, you've often promised to, but you never seem to get round to it. Have a drink and tell me about him.

Don't mind if I do. The mosquitoes were bad last night.

What's that got to do with it?

Oh, nothing—just that I can't stand mosquitoes. It's not so much the sting as that buzzing noise they make.

There's no mosquitoes out my way, so I don't have to worry. Here's your beer. What did this old age pensioner do again?

Couldn't sleep a wink all night with mosquitoes buzzing about and stinging me.

Why don't you get some of that DDT spray? It's sudden death to mosquitoes, I've heard.

But I think these are Northern Territory mosquitoes.

What? Do you think they flew two thousand miles just to bite you? Anyway, what difference would it make?

DDT has no effect on Northern Territory mosquitoes. The mossies are big in the Territory.

Must be.

Not that you'd notice. One time a big mosquito landed on the tarmac at Darwin airport and they pumped fifty gallons of petrol into it thinking it was an aeroplane. The mosquitoes are the reason why the place has such a small population.

I thought the low rainfall and poor soil were the cause of it.

Have you ever been in the Territory?

Never.

Then how would you know? There was an old age pensioner one time who died after being attacked by a swarm of mosquitoes in the Territory.

You don't tell!

Positive fact. If you don't believe me ask Truthful Jones. The mosquitoes hunted him out of the Territory, so he ought to know.

How did that come to happen?

Well, they're big and tough, like I said, and they don't like the white man taking the Territory off the aborigines.

Now I've heard everything.

You never heard of a mosquito biting a blackfellow in the Territory, did you?

Can't say I have.

Well, what did I tell you. If the mosquitoes have their way, there won't be a white man in the Territory in twenty years.

Listen, are you going to tell me about that old age pensioner or not?

Who brought up the subject of mosquitoes, anyway?

You did.

Well, what do you expect, when they kept me awake all night?

I expect you to tell me about that old age pensioner. . . . Have another drink and get on with the story.

It's a strange thing: they put an aboriginal in jail if he buys another fella a drink.

Yes, it's a disgrace. Here's your beer.

Thanks. You've got to hand it to the Northern Territory mosquitoes, they treat the aborigines well. The aborigines used to use them for transport when they were hunting birds, in the days before the white man came.

The Australian aborigines never domesticated animals or tilled the soil—and I'm sure they didn't use mosquitoes for transport.

I must admit I didn't believe it myself when Truthful Jones told me, but he ought to know because . . .

—because the mosquitoes hunted him out of the Territory. . . .

Actually, they *carried* him out. . . .

All right! How did they manage it?

Well, old Truthful copped it from those mosquitoes, I can tell you, on account he was a white man. Didn't get a wink of sleep for six months.

Why didn't he use a mosquito net over his bed?

He did, but the mossies used to form up like dive bombers and swoop under the sides of the net.

Why didn't he tuck the sides in?

He did but then they used to form a straight line so their proboscis points acted like a big knife and cut a hole in the net for them to fly through.

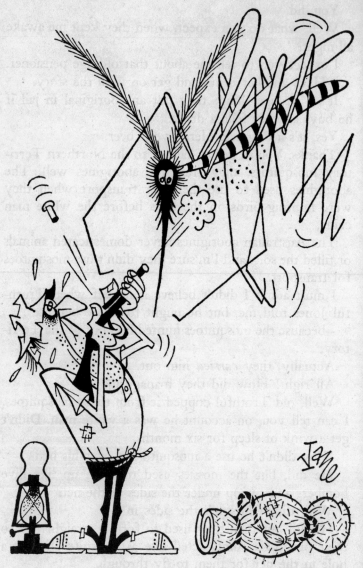

"... Sawn off shot-gun but they didn't turn a hair!"

—Would have a powerful proboscis, a mosquito as big as that.

You can say that again; like a hypodermic needle usually used to give injections to sick elephants. Strange word proboscis, isn't it? I knew a poet one time who told me it is the only word in the English language that won't rhyme with any other. But he solved it; he wrote a poem called "There was a young man from Damoscis, who fractured his proboscis."

The word is Damascus.

A case of poetic licence, he reckoned.

It seems you are a great believer in poetic licence.

Truthful Jones didn't believe in it. A stickler for the truth, he was. If he told a story and people didn't believe it, he'd get upset and go off his tucker. Like when he told me that the Northern Territory aborigines used to ride mosquitoes when they went hunting and use the proboscis for stabbing kangaroos and eagles, in the days before the white man came. He got real upset when I didn't believe him.

You don't mean to say.

Positive fact—didn't eat for a week. Anyway, as I was saying before you so rudely interrupted, the mosquitoes are big in the Territory. Their stings brought out lumps on Truthful Jones as big as tennis balls. He tried everything to get a bit of sleep; DDT, poison gas, and a sawn off shot-gun, but they didn't turn a hair. So, one night, he thought of a bright idea: instead of going to bed, he took his mattress and blankets and a hammer and got into a big iron tank that was empty on account of the dry season.

Why the hammer?

Well, he knew the mossies would find him and attack

with their pro—what's-their-names—and try to cut a hole in the tank. And he was right. They attacked one at a time at first, and every time a proboscis stuck through he bent it with a hammer. A shrewd old head was Truthful.

Must have been.

You can say that again. But then the rest of the mossies had a conference and decided to attack in dive bomber formation. And *zoom*!—a row of proboscises stuck through shaped liked a "V". And old Truthful bent them over with his hammer. Well, the mossies brought up reinforcements and Truthful heard them talking outside the tank. . . .

Just a minute, do you expect me . . .

No, I don't expect you to believe that Northern Territory mosquitoes can speak English but, you see, Truthful had picked up a smattering of their particular lingo, an aboriginal dialect, needless to say. And he heard them planning to form their proboscises into a hacksaw to cut a hole in the tank. And *zoom*! they attacked in a line. But Truthful was too quick for them. He bent each proboscis in turn with his hammer, like playing a tune on a xylophone. And pretty soon every mosquito in the area was caught by the nose in the walls of the tank.

I believe you—but millions wouldn't.

You can ask old Truthful Jones. He didn't get his nickname for nothing. Anyway, he was very weary seeing as he hadn't slept for six months. So he soon fell sound asleep. And when he woke up the tank was on the banks of the Yarra River in Melbourne two thousand miles away. Truthful Jones never went back to the Territory after that.

Don't blame him. Have another drink and tell me about that old age pensioner.

Ah, that story sounds a bit exaggerated. You wouldn't believe it. And I'm like Truthful Jones: I can't stand people who don't believe my stories. Anyway, I've got to go now.

What's your hurry?

Well, I want to buy a hammer before the shops shut. I'm thinking of sleeping in an iron tank tonight.

5

How Sam Loxton was Caught
at Square Leg

(as told by Billy Borker in
Young and Jackson's Hotel, Melbourne)

B<small>EEN</small> listening to the cricket, mate?
Yes.
The game's not what it was.
Oh, I don't know.
The game's too slow now, mate. The batsmen won't
have a go. Not like in the old days of Bradman and
Ponsford and McCabe. And Sam Loxton. There was
a cricketer. You remember Sam?

A good all rounder, Sam.

You can say that again. One of the best. An attacking batsman; always looking for runs. But we trapped
him. Did I ever tell you how Sam Loxton was caught
at square leg?

Don't think you did. Have a drink and tell me about
it.

At a place Benson's Valley it happened during the
war. Sam Loxton was in the army stationed in a camp
near by. Someday, someone ought to make a list of
things ruined by war—including the careers of a lot
of good cricketers. Take Ken Mueleman, for instance.

34

I thought your story was about Sam Loxton.

So it is. But I'm using Ken Mueleman as an example of my argument. Just at the peak of his form when war broke out. Then came five years with no cricket to speak of. Same thing would have happened to Sam Loxton. There he is in an army camp at Benson's Valley out of practice. So he gets in touch with the local cricket association. "What about a friendly match?" he says. "The competition's closed down," they told him. "All the cricketers are in the army." Sam was determined. "Couldn't you scratch a side together to play a team from the army camp?" Well, seeing it was Sam Loxton they did their best and fielded a team of old cricketers and soldiers on leave. A one-day game from eleven o'clock till six o'clock on a Saturday.

So Sam kept in practice?

But we trapped him at square leg. I was bowling myself at the time, so I ought to know. Anyway Benson's Valley won the toss and batted. Made about a hundred and fifty. Then the army team goes in. Sam Loxton opened up himself. Wanted to get plenty of practice. He went for a hit and played for the strike. A good attacking batsman, Sam, not like the powderpuff cricketers these days. By four o'clock, the army had passed the local team's score—but Sam wanted more practice. Now, at that time, the greatest cricket umpire Australia ever saw lived in Benson's Valley, name of Arty McConkidale. Knew the rule book off by heart. When he sat for his examinations for umpiring, Jack Ryder and all the experts tried to trick him but they weren't in the hunt. Got the highest pass ever in the exams. Would have been a test umpire only he was too fond of the gargle. The gargle has ruined many a good man. His father was a good umpire, too, but fond of the gargle, just like his son.

What has this got to do with trapping Sam Loxton at square leg?

Got a lot to do with it. They were umpiring this day. And they began to get terrible thirsty. Nearly a hundred in the shade, it was. Anyway, by five o'clock, Sam Loxton's team was more than a hundred in front with only seven wickets down. So I said to Sam: "Why don't you retire or declare the innings closed? The umpires are getting thirsty and the pubs shut at six." "I need all the practice I can get," Sam told me, "and the game doesn't finish until six o'clock." Well we played on and managed to get two of the tail-enders out. Only one more wicket to fall. But Sam Loxton kept playing for the strike. Hitting us all over the ground, he was. I bowled him a short one outside the leg stump. He stepped right across and pulled it round to leg. The ball went like a rocket straight at Arty McConkidale, umpiring at square leg. He was standing there thinking, the pubs will be closed before they get him out. He had four cricket caps on his head, three white jumpers tied around his neck by the sleeves, a couple of watches on each wrist. The ball was coming straight at his face. He put his hands up and caught it.

Hey, wait a minute. . . .

"How's that?" I appealed to Arty's father, who was umpiring at the bowler's end. He hesitated, licked his lips then raised his finger. "Out," he said. And he lifted the bails and headed straight towards the pub. His son shook the caps, jumpers, and watches into a heap on the grass and followed him. The two teams went, too, leaving

Sam Loxton standing in the middle of the pitch wondering what rule he'd been given out under.

First I ever heard of an umpire catching a batsman out.

You live and learn. We had a lot more friendly games, but Sam Loxton always brought his own umpires, after that.

6

Pianists are Made Not Born

(as told by Billy Borker in the
Globe Hotel, Brisbane)

I'M very fond of piano music.

Got a piano?

Yes, I bought one second-hand—last week, as a matter of fact.

Pity I hadn't known. A few years ago I could have got you a brand new Steinway grand worth more than a thousand pounds for a song.

This sounds like another story. Have a drink and tell me about it.

I'll force one down just to be sociable. The story is called: pianists are made not born. There was this passenger ship being built at Cockatoo Dock in Sydney, see. A'course, the waterfront police kept a sharp lookout for thieves.

There must be a lot of thieves in Sydney.

According to the Melbourne people there are. Anyway, one night they get a call to say the brand new Steinway grand piano has disappeared from the first class saloon. So they send two of their best men down. The saloon is at the top of the spiral staircase, they tell them. One of the detectives rings back from the ship. "What spiral staircase," he says. "We can't find no spiral staircase."

Here's your beer.

Thanks. Not a bad pub this. See that old alco over there. They call him Sputnik—always going around the Globe.

But who would steal a spiral staircase?

I don't rightly know—but a fella named Light Fingers Jackson from Woolloomooloo stole the Steinway grand piano. He went out in a boat with his mate in the middle of the night, grabbed the grand goanna and lowered it down in a lifeboat, see. They get ashore, load the piano on a truck and hide it in the shed behind Light Fingers' house.

Be a hard thing to sell, a Steinway grand. . . .

Wait till I tell you. They go to a fence, see, a receiver of stolen goods named Octopus McGillicuddy. But the old Octopus wouldn't have a bar of it: "Do you know how many Steinway grands there are in the whole of Sydney? About a dozen. Want me to get arrested? That piano's as hot as the hobs of hell." Well, Light Fingers Jackson and his mate get their thinking caps on, and decide to telephone to professors of music and concert pianists. They started off asking for five hundred quid, but no takers. People were suspicious, like, you know how it is. So they drop the price to two hundred and start peddling the piano around the clubs. Still no takers. And the police are out everywhere looking and the papers full of the mystery of the missing piano. Next they drop the price to a hundred quid and try the pubs. Ten o'clock closing had just come in and the publicans were bringing on a bit of a floor show—still no takers. And, boy, was that piano getting hot? A big reward was offered. Light Fingers and his mate were getting nervous. . . .

But you said this story was called pianists are made not born. I don't see . . .

Barley Charley. My father always said, never get ahead of your story. At last, in desperation, they drop the price to fifty quid and start ringing up clubs in the bush. But nobody would touch that piano with a forty-foot pole. "Only one thing to do," Light Fingers' mate said. "You'll have to learn to play it yourself."

"Play it nothing," Light Fingers says. "I'm going to get rid of it." "How?" his mate asks. "Give it away, that's how, and quick, before we get nabbed with it." So they offer the Steinway grand to the local publican. "What's wrong with it?" he asks; "must be something wrong with it, if you're giving it away." The same wherever they went; people wouldn't take it as a present. They ran around like a forger with a million dollar cheque. They rang up students and orphanages and convents—but nobody would take the piano.

I still can't see what this has to do with pianists being made not born.

Well, one night late, they sneak the Steinway grand piano out of the shed, on to the truck and away they go. They drive around for a while, then turn into a dead end slum street and dump it there. Next morning, Light Fingers buys the papers but there's nothing about the piano. That afternoon, he buys the papers again. "We'll read all about it," he tells his mate. But there was not a word. And Light Fingers and his mate never saw or heard of the piano again from that day to this.

Hey, I wonder whatever did become of that piano.

Well, I heard afterwards, that there was an unemployed fella living in that street, had a large family, poor as a church mouse. One of his kids was a very promising pianist but he couldn't afford to buy a piano for him to practise on. Imagine how he felt when he came out at dawn and saw there before his eyes—a Steinway grand piano. Well, he takes a look around, calls his missus and they drag it into the house.

The plot thickens.

That little kid practised six hours a day on that piano and he got so good that a professor from the Conservatorium gave him free lessons. I won't mention any names, but he's one of Australia's greatest pianists today. It's like I told you, pianists are made not born.

7

How the Melbourne-Sydney Argument was Settled

(as told by Billy Borker in Boden's Hotel, Albury)

Dᴵᴰ you have a bet on the Melbourne Cup?

That would be the last race I'd bet on.

Why's that?

Too big a field and too many triers. Anyway, it would be better if the Melbourne Cup was never run. It causes too many arguments between Melbourne and Sydney people about horses and jockeys.

It's funny how Melbourne and Sydney people always argue, isn't it?

Actually, we settled the Melbourne-Sydney argument on neutral territory, one time. Did I ever tell you about it?

No, have another drink and tell me.

Don't mind if I do. It happened right here in this pub, near the Victorian and New South Wales border —neutral territory. There were these two blokes: one from Melbourne, the other from Sydney. They were the best of mates, fought in the war together, worked together, drank together—but used to argue about Melbourne and Sydney.

Of course, these arguments are only a joke.

They start off as a joke, like between these two blokes I'm telling you about, Melbourne Mick and Sydney Sam. But they often get serious I can tell you. They might start making sly little jokes about the harbour bridge being an oversized coathanger, or the Yarra the only river in the world that flows upside down. Melbourne Mick would say: "The only city in the world where they have a public holiday for a horse race."

And Sydney Sam would come back: "But more Sydney than Melbourne jockeys have ridden the Cup winner in the last ten years." So they'd switch to jockeys. Sydney Sam would talk about George Moore riding more winners every season than any Melbourne jockey. And Melbourne Mick would quote how Scobie Breasley won the English jockey's premiership two years in a row. So they'd switch to horses and go at it hammer and tongs. Melbourne Mick would end up quoting Phar Lap's record; and Sydney Sam would refer to Tulloch's stake winnings. Well, I used to drink with them, see, and I was a neutral in the Melbourne-Sydney war. So I'd say: "Both Phar Lap and Tulloch are New Zealand bred horses."

So that's how you settled the argument?

It wasn't that easy, mate. No, they come to blows more than once about football. Melbourne Mick would say: "Australian Rules draws bigger crowds in Melbourne than Rugby in Sydney." "What?" Sydney Sam would say, "that's not football, mate, it's aerial ping-pong." That aerial ping-pong crack was always good for a fight in the pub yard. After the fight, Melbourne Mick would start the argument again. "In Rugby they throw the ball all the time. A good Australian Rules player would kick a goal on a Rugby ground from the other end." Then I would intervene, see. "Hang on a minute, don't either of you realise that the only true game of football is soccer? They use the feet only, *real* football."

That should have settled that one?

Settled nothing. They'd get on to climate. Sydney Sam would make a sarcastic remark about it always raining in Melbourne; and Melbourne Mick would say he'd read in the paper where there was more sunny days a year in Melbourne than Sydney. They had three or four fights about the weather. So I wrote to that weather station in Queensland and got back a letter to say that Sydney actually had a higher rainfall than Melbourne but that Melbourne had less sunny days than Sydney.

That should have satisfied them?

No. They changed the subject to migration. I thought Melbourne Mick had Sydney Sam over the barrel. He proved on official figures that Melbourne attracted more migrants than Sydney. But old Sydney Sam said this was due to more migrants from London going to Melbourne. "And what's that got to do with it?" Melbourne Mick asked. "Well, the Thames is muddy, just like the Yarra." And out into the pub yard they went again.

Terrible thing to see two friends fighting like that.

It worried me, I can tell you. But I gradually broke them down on the Yarra and the bridge, horses and jockeys, football, climate and migration. And on the question of population I broke up a fight by explaining that, while Sydney had the bigger population Melbourne was growing faster.

"A terrible thing to see two friends fighting . . . !"

You should have been a diplomat.

It took more than a diplomat to stop them arguing about beer, mate. They had a fight every pay night about beer. This pub, being on the border, served both Melbourne and Sydney beer, in those days. Melbourne Mick drank Melbourne beer and Sydney Sam drank Sydney beer, needless to say. And they'd needle each other. "Melbourne beer has a higher alcoholic content," Mick would say. "That's why there's more alcoholics in Melbourne than Sydney," Sam would reply. "Sydney beer is thick and frothy like a milk shake," Melbourne Mick would argue. "Everybody knows Melbourne beer is the best. Some say it's because the water's more suitable." This would give Sam an opening. "I always knew Melbourne beer was watered." That was good for another fight. I tried everything to stop them. Even got the barman to serve Mick Sydney beer and Sam Melbourne beer.

That would settle it!

Not on your life. They knew the difference. They each took one sip, spat it out and said: "What, are you trying to poison me?" They had so many fights I was worried they would end up punchy. So one night I says to them: "Listen, mates, these arguments and fights over Melbourne and Sydney beer have got to stop. Tell you what I'll do. I'll send a sample of the best Melbourne and Sydney beer to the C.S.I.R.O. for analysis. Will you abide by their decision?"

That was a bright idea.

Well, Mick and Sam were both of a scientific turn of mind, as you can see. So they agreed: if the C.S.I.R.O. said both beers were excellent that would end the argument. "And," I says, "if they say one beer is better than the other, you have to accept the decision." They couldn't have agreed quicker. So I got a bottle of best Melbourne and Sydney beer, scraped the labels off, marked them A and B and sent them off with a letter to the C.S.I.R.O.

And what did the C.S.I.R.O. say?

Weeks went by and we got no reply. Melbourne Mick and Sydney Sam began to argue and sometimes fight over the likely result of the test.

So I sent a telegram to the C.S.I.R.O. And back came the answer: "Thorough tests made—stop—regret inform you both horses have yellow jaundice." That's how we settled the argument between Melbourne and Sydney.

8

The Sundowner who Paid his Fare
out of Wagga Wagga

(as told by Billy Borker in the
Royal Hotel, Bacchus Marsh)

Dᴵᴰ I ever tell you about the sundowner who paid
his fare out of Wagga Wagga?

A new story, eh? Let's have it.

I never tell new stories, mate. I let my stories mature
like good beer.

It's good wine that matures.

Easy seeing you don't go to the gee-gees.

What's that got to do with it?

Racecourse beer isn't mature—it's made that morning.
Punters will put up with anything—except dead favour-
ites.

Tell us about the sundowner. What did he do again?

Paid his fare on a train out of Wagga Wagga.

What's unusual about that?

What? Sundowners never pay fares. It's against the
rules of the Bagmen's Union.

Bagmen's Union? Never heard of it.

Easy to see you weren't on the track during the
Depression. Would you believe that I wore herring
tins for shoes once? And my wife Clara—who always

liked to put on side—wore condensed milk tins for high heels?

You're pulling my leg again. I never met your wife Clara, you know.

That's because of the stupid drinking laws in this country. You drink with your mates in the pub and your wife at home, and never the twain shall meet. You'd like old Clara. She stuck to me during the Depression and I stick to her now.

This happened during the Depression, did it?

No, just after the war. It happened this way. I joined the army when war broke out. Came straight off the track. The Sixth Divvy was made up mainly of bagmen; first steady job we ever had was getting shot at. I joined up with Timetable Tommy.

Timetable Tommy? What's he got to do with the story?

Don't look down your nose at old Timetable Tommy. A very cultured man: knew the time every train left every town in four states.

You were going to tell me about an old sundowner.

Well, me and Timetable got discharged from the army in Queensland in 1946. We had more than four hundred quid each in the kick, but seeing as we hadn't paid a train fare since 1930, we jumped the rattler out of Brisbane by force of habit. We got to Albury easy enough and was aiming to take the Spirit of Progress on the run, but she's hard, the Spirit, so we decided to hitch-hike down the highway. . . .

Where does the old sundowner come into it?

I was just about to tell you, mate, but you keep interrupting. We came on him sitting under a pepper-

49

corn tree at Wodonga. And do you know what he was doing?

I haven't any idea.

So help me—he's grilling a nice bit of T-bone steak on one of them there wire grillers.

You don't tell.

Positive fact. Corks on his hat brim, a scraggy beard, about fourpence worth of old clothes on, eyes staring like holes burned in a blanket. "Where did you get the flash griller, mate?" I asked him. "Bought it at the iron-monger's in Albury," he says. "That's a nice bit of steak," Timetable Tommy says. "I bought it at the but-cher's," the sundowner tells him. "Struth," Tommy says, "things have changed on the track: sundowners paying for steak and grillers." "You been on the track?" the sundowner asks. "Yeh, before the war," Timetable replies; "Bit different then—you were lucky to get a handout of maggoty mutton." Anyway, the old fella gives us a bit of steak and we hoe in. "The track's not what it was," he tells us, "people offering you work. You get handouts of cash sometimes. And I paid me fare on a train yesterday—first time in forty years." Timetable Tommy was shocked, I can tell you. "That's against the rules of the Bagmen's Union," he says. "How-ever did you come to do a thing like that?"

How did he come to do it? That's the point I'm waiting for.

Well, it happened this way. The old sundowner told us he was up at Wagga Wagga asleep under a bridge when a farmer woke him up and said: "Do you want a job harvesting?" "Not me," he tells him, "it's against me principles." "Ten quid a week and your keep," the farmer begged, "and a forty-hour week." The old sun-downer was just getting to sleep again when another cocky comes down the bank. "Do you want a job, old man?" "No, thanks," he said, "it's against the Union Rules. Go away and let a man sleep." "Fifteen pound a week and your keep," the farmer said, "double time for Saturdays and sleep in the house with sheets on the bed." Well, Timetable Tommy got upset again: "Bit different from the old days," he said. "Ten bob a week and sleep in the barn with the rats."

What about the sundowner paying his fare?

I'm telling you the story the way the sundowner told me and Timetable Tommy. He decided to brew a billy of tea then push off. He was just lighting his fire when up drove a car and out got a cocky in leggings and riding breeches. "Sorry to disturb you, old son," he said, "would you care for employment during the harvest? Twenty pounds a week and the use of my car at weekends." The old sundowner was beginning to weaken. He no sooner got rid of that cocky when up drove another one, in a Rolls-Royce, and a beaut sheila with him. The old sundowner thought to him-self: "What's goin' on? If I stay here I'll end up taking a job." So he rolls up his swag and legs it up the opp-osite bank and down to the railway station for the lick of his life. The passenger train was about to pull out. Too late to jump it. So the old sundowner had to pay his fare, for the first time for forty years.

The lesser of two evils?

Yeh. Me and Timetable Tommy asked him: "And where are you going now, old-timer?" "To the Strze-lecki Ranges until after the harvest," he told us, "noth-ing grows there except gum trees and bracken."

Does that story have a moral?

The moral is, mate, that there's either a famine or a feast, and that prosperity's no good unless you know how to use it.

Nothing wrong with prosperity.

Trouble with this country today is that people don't know how to use the prosperity they've got. Spending all their money on poker machines, household gadgets, slow horses, fast cars, Beatle wigs, and beer.

9

Money Doesn't Make Much Difference

(as told by Billy Borker in
Hosie's Hotel, Melbourne)

I'M nearly broke again; don't know where the money
goes.

Money doesn't make much difference. If you've
got your health you've got everything.

I guess you're right, but I wish I knew how to make
some big money.

The only time I worry about money is when I
haven't got any. And right now, if roast turkey were
a penny an ounce, I couldn't afford a feather of a
tomtit's tail.

It's no fun being broke.

Being broke's not the worst of it. No man's so poor
he can't get into debt. Being in debt is a way of life in
this country. Do you know that every Australian owes
about five hundred quid to the National Debt and fifty
quid to the hire purchase companies? Makes you think,
don't it?

Ah, there's great opportunities for making money in
this country.

You've got to have money to make money, mate,
that's the trouble. You know what the old Bible said:

"To the haves shall be given and the have-nots shall be touched for their last penny."

I don't seem to recall reading *that* in the Bible.

Well, words to that effect, anyway.

I still say there's money to be made in this country, if you work hard.

One thing you can depend on, mate, is that those who work hardest earn the least.

I read in the paper several times about men who started with nothing becoming millionaires.

Don't believe everything you read in the paper; it's like I said, money doesn't make much difference.

I've never noticed you throwing it around.

What! I won the lottery once and spent the lot in six months. That's how it is with the Australian battler. If he gets hold of big money, he thinks it'll last forever, so he gets rid of it quick. He sticks to his mates, doesn't become a snob or anything like that, but pretty soon he's broke again.

Surely you've heard of a man who made money and hung on to it?

Yeh, I have, come to think of it. But it didn't make much difference to him. A fella by the name of Sheckles Mitchell.

You always have a specific character in your stories.

That's because they're true, mate. Had a head on him like a burglar's torch.

A burglar's torch?

Yeh, a long thin neck and a round head. Every real character has a definite name and a head on him like something. I'll tell this story my way, see. But if you tell it to someone else, you can use a different name and say his head was like something else: maybe a robber's dog or a warped sandshoe.

But I thought you said the stories are true.

Every Australian yarn is true—for the yarn-spinner who tells it, that's what my father always reckoned. Well, this fella Sheckles Mitchell was always trying to make money. Believed all the stories about office boys becoming managing directors. He tried everything: selling gum leaves, hot dogs, home-made pickles, insurance policies, vacuum cleaners, encyclopaedias, and second-hand cars. He tried SP betting, interstate truck driving, and chicken sexing. But he couldn't get in front.

You said he eventually made money.

Yeh. It was a funny thing. He could never keep creases in his trousers.

And what's that got to do with it?

Got a lot to do with it. His missus used to nag him about it. He tried everything, even putting his trousers under the mattress at night. Then he hit on an idea. A special trouser hanger that would keep the creases in your trousers.

You don't tell.

Positive fact. He invented this here trouser hanger and began to manufacture them in a shed in his back-yard. He put 'em on the market and they sold like hot cakes—that was before they invented these here stove pipe trousers without creases. Anyway, pretty soon he had a factory and ten women working for him.

What'd I tell you?

That's the secret, mate, get other people working for you. Anyway, he gets an accountant to work out how much money he is making and one day he comes home

55

and says to his missus: "Now, darling, I've got money. The accountant says I'm well in front. Is there anything you want?" "No, dear, all I want is you and the children." "I insist," he says, "you stuck to me during the Depression. Now I've got money, you can have anything you want." "Well," his missus says, "there *is* one thing. Everyone in the street has got a barbecue in their backyard." "Say no more," he tells her, "get one put in right away. The best in the street." So they get the barbecue put it.

Great idea, a barbecue.

Well, next June he comes home and tells his wife that the accountant has declared another dividend. "Just say the word, if there's anything you want," he says. "Well darling, there *is* just one more thing." "Name it," he says. "Well," his missus tells him, "having the didee in the backyard isn't very convenient," the wife says. "How right you are," he tells her; "get the plumbers in and build the best toilet that money can buy, right inside the house. Tiled walls, the lot. Spare no expense."

A man who spent his money wisely!

You can say that again. Trouble was he got that way he could talk about nothing else except money. Used to get on his mates' nerves down at the club—always bashing their ear about how much money he was making, about having shares in the B.H.P., a barbecue in the backyard and a didee in the house. Kept it up, day in and day out. One of his mates got sick of this, see. So he says to Sheckles Mitchell, "Listen Sheckles," he says, "you are always yak-yaking about how much money you're making. What difference has all this money made?" Well, the old Sheckles thinks for a minute, looks a bit puzzled then says: "Well, it hasn't made much difference at all, really. Before I had money I used to eat in the house and the didee was in the backyard. Now I eat in the backyard and the didee's in the house. Come to think of it, money doesn't make much difference."

10

There's No Certainties in Racing or the Needy and the Greedy

(as told by Billy Borker in the
Seven Seas Hotel, Newcastle)

GOOD DAY, Mister Borker!
What's this Mister Borker business? You can call me Billy.

Thanks, Billy. My name's, er, Jerome, Jerome Smith! A bloke gave me a tip yesterday. Said it was a certainty and it didn't even run a place.

There's no certainties in racing, young Jerome.

First bet I ever had.

Make it the last. Only two kinds of people punt the horses, the needy and the greedy. You're not needy and you shouldn't be greedy.

You a punter yourself?

Used to be, but I gave up keeping bookmakers years ago. A mug's game.

Oh, it's a good sport, I reckon.

It's not a sport mate, it's a lottery with four-legged tickets.

I saw an advertisement in the paper the other day for a foolproof system. Only ten pounds. Guaranteed to win ten thousand a year.

What? Do you think a bloke would sell a system that could win that kind of money? He'd keep it locked in a safe, if it was fair dinkum.

There must be some system.

They all send you broke in the long run. More blokes gone bankrupt and more bank clerks tickled the peter through following systems, and listening to tips, than you could poke a stick at.

Some blokes beat the game, I hear.

Only bookmakers—and crushers.

What's a crusher?

A crusher's a bloke who backs a horse at, say, five to one; then lays it in a bookmaker's bag, at say three to one. Has two points going to nothing.

I don't quite follow.

The less *you* learn about horse racing the better.

I got a telegram from a bloke in Melbourne last week offering to sell me a special tip every Saturday for a fiver.

So the smarties have got you on a mugs' list. News travels fast.

Mugs' list?

Yeh. These tipsters gradually build up a list of people who are mugs enough to pay for tips.

Fancy that now. You reckon there's no way to pick winners?

Reckon? I'm sure. Unless you could buy the Sunday papers on Saturday morning.

And bet after the results.

Yeh. The only way to be sure to win would be to bet after the race. A funny thing, that chance was once offered to a thousand punters. Did I ever tell you about the two tipsters who offered their clients a bet on a winner—after the race?

Have another drink, and tell me about it.

Don't mind if I do. Well, these two tipsters, Black Snowy and Integrity Hanson were going bad, see.

Black Snowy and Integrity Hanson? You get some rare nicknames.

All Australian nicknames have a reason: Black Snowy had white hair and jet-black eyebrows. And Integrity Hanson was a man of integrity—he stuck with great integrity to the smarties' principle: never give a sucker an even break. Anyway, things were crook in Tallarook with them, at the time. Even the mugs on their own mugs' list stopped buying their tips. So one day, Black Snowy says: "They wouldn't buy our tips if we sent a winner—after the race was over." And this gives old Integrity the idea of the century. "Black Snowy, old mate," he says, "you're a genius." "It's not my fault," Black Snowy tells him. "Seriously, mate," Integrity gets carried away, "some of the mugs on our list would fall for it. I'll draft a telegram." Our — special — Saturday Hairylegs — won — five — to — one — stop — Forgot — inform — you — stop — As — valuable — client — can now — place — bet — after — race — stop — strict — limit — ten — pounds — stop — Cash — or — telegram — Money — order — no — cheques — stop — Integrity — Box 999 G.P.O.

But you don't mean to tell me . . .

If you don't believe me you can ask Integrity Hanson. They invested their last money in a thousand telegrams. And when they went to the post office they had to bring a suitcase to carry the letters and telegrams away. Five hundred tenners in two days. Five thousand quid.

So up they choof to the travel agency and buy two one-way air tickets to Mexico on a plane.

Got away with five thousand, eh?

Like I told you. The needy and the greedy. They are in the pub opposite the post office having a last swig of Australian beer before they catch the plane, when Black Snowy says: "It fair breaks me heart to think that over there in the box there's another bundle of tenners just waiting to be picked up." But old Integrity was cautious: "Some mug is bound to squeal coppers sooner or later. We agreed to stop at five thousand quid." Black Snowy pleaded: "Just one more trip across the road." Well, Integrity Hanson weakened and over they go. He was just about to put the key in the lock of Box 999 when three big detectives appear out of the gloom and charge them with fraud and conspiracy.

They'd get a long stretch for a charge like that.

Integrity Hanson was a bit of a bush lawyer. He conducted their defence. After the police and a few of the mugs gave evidence, he made a speech that will ring down through legal history. He says: "Your Honour, they don't call me Integrity Hanson for nothing. We had every intention of paying these people at the odds of five to one, we were just ready to sign the cheques, but now that aspersions have been cast on our character we are only going to refund their money."

Don't tell me they got off!

Yeh, they had to refund all the money though. Let that be a lesson to you, mate; there's no certainties in racing.

II

The Crookest Raffle Ever Run in Australia

(as told by Billy Borker in the
James Ruse Hotel, Rouse Hill)

Dᴵᴰ I ever tell yer about the crookest raffle ever
run in Australia?

No, but you told me about the only fair
dinkum one.

That's a different raffle altogether. That's the one I
ran at Woolloomooloo during the Depression.

You'd better have a drink.

Don't mind if I do. Well, this here raffle I'm talking
about was for a pumpkin and it was run in a place
called Benson's Valley. It was run by a fella called
Trigger MacIntosh. Don't know how he got that nickname but I know he had thirteen kids. Little fella. Bald
as a billiard ball.

But people wouldn't buy a ticket in a raffle for a
pumpkin surely.

Australians will buy a raffle ticket in anything. They
got into the habit during the Depression. Buying raffle
tickets is like going to church or drinking beer, once
you get into the habit. . . . Anyway, this was a special
pumpkin. The biggest pumpkin ever grown in the
history of the world. It was so big it took six men six
hours to dig it out of the ground.

But pumpkins don't grow under the ground.

I know that, but this one was so heavy it sunk into the ground till you couldn't see it.

You don't say.

If you don't believe me you can ask Trigger MacIntosh. He grew that pumpkin, brother. I'm telling you: it took six men six hours to dig . . .

You told me that.

Yeh, but it took the same six men another six hours to roll it up six planks on to a six-ton truck to take it to the pub to be raffled. But my father always said: "Never get ahead of your story." So first I must tell you how they came to grow this here pumpkin.

They? But you said this bloke grew it himself. What did you say his name was?

Trigger MacIntosh. Matter of fact, Trigger didn't grow this pumpkin at all. He owned it in partnership with another fella—name of Greenfingers Stratton. Old Greenfingers could grow a crop of show orchids on a concrete footpath, so my father reckoned. Well, one day Trigger said to Greenfingers: "I know where I can borrow a block of land and start a market garden." Fancy mentioning a block of land to old Greenfingers— always saying "If only I had a block of land, I'd grow somethin', I can tell yer." Funny how people never fulfil their ambitions. I knew a violinist once who wanted to be a League footballer. . . .

You've told me about him. Have another drink and get on with your story. . . .

Well, it turned out that Trigger had talked an old cocky with more money than sense into lending him some land on the river bank. Very rich soil from the floods that happened every few years. A good mags-

63

man was Trigger; would have made a fortune in Parliament, I can tell you. Well, they decided to grow pumpkins, for some reason, and Greenfingers went to work. Pretty soon pumpkin vines began to crawl all over the property, across the creek, over some paddocks of lucerne, up the side of the cocky's house and down the road towards the pub. Well, anyhow, Trigger and Greenfingers waited for the pumpkins to grow but nothing happened until one day one solitary pumpkin began to grow right in the middle of the paddock. It grew so fast you could see it bulging. It became so heavy it began to sink into the ground. And eventually it took six men . . .

Yes, I know, six men six hours to dig it out.

That's right, and the same six men another six hours to roll it up six planks on to a six-ton truck to take it down to the pub.

All right. Why didn't they sell the pumpkin or enter it in the Royal Show?

What? Made a lot of money raffling it six times— that's why! Anyway down to the pub they went with it. A'course, it wouldn't fit in the pub door, needless to say, so they left it on the truck outside. And Trigger put a sign on it: THE BIGGEST PUMPKIN EVER GREW—6d. A TICKET. Bought six raffle books at the newsagent's with a hundred tickets in each. . . .

Did they sell all the tickets?

For sure! In the pub. The pumpkin being so big and people being in the habit of buying raffle tickets, like I told you. There was a crowd around that pumpkin all day outside the Royal Hotel and during the afternoon six blokes got on top of it and sat in the sun

"It became so heavy it began to sink!"

drinking beer. Just before closing time, the raffle was drawn.

Who won it?

Old Greenfingers himself, naturally, seeing Trigger drew the ticket out of the kerosene tin he had for the purpose and seeing it was the crookest raffle ever run in Australia, as I said before. Eventually they raffled the pumpkin six times. If you don't believe me you can ask Trigger MacIntosh. . . .

And I suppose this bloke Greenfingers won it every time?

No, he only won it five times.

Well, who won it the other time? One of these days someone is going to kill you right in the middle of one of your stories.

Trouble with you is, you try to ruin a story by making me get ahead of myself. My father always said . . .

Yeh, I know what he always said . . . here's your beer.

Thanks. Well, now, to tell the story properly. Greenfingers Stratton won the first raffle on account of Trigger MacIntosh had a ticket with a secret mark on it. Anyway, the next Saturday they brought the pumpkin back to the pub again.

Be a bit awkward wouldn't it? Raffling the biggest pumpkin ever grew more than once.

Matterafact, they changed the sign to read "THE SECOND BIGGEST PUMPKIN EVER GREW", and sold six hundred tickets again and old Greenfingers won it. The next Saturday, they raffled the third biggest pumpkin ever grew, and so on, until they arrived at the pub one Saturday morning with the sixth biggest pumpkin ever grew.

You don't mean to say . . .

If you don't believe me, you can ask Greenfingers. . . .

I believe you but thousands wouldn't. Go on; who won it the sixth time?

Needless to say, that there pumpkin was becoming a bit the worse for wear what with rolling it on and off the truck, and people climbing up on to it to drink their beer. It was bruised and battered, so my father reckoned. Trigger MacIntosh said afterwards it seemed to have a face and used to snarl at him when he walked past it. Now, for some reason certain people, wowsers and the like, started to say the raffles weren't fair dinkum.

You don't tell me.

It's a fact. There's no pleasing some people. Anyhow, my father reckoned that Danny O'Connell, the publican, said to Trigger: "Listen, that there sixth biggest pumpkin that ever grew. I seem to have seen it somewhere before." "A simple case of mistaken identity," Trigger told him. He was as quick as a flash, was Trigger. Did I ever tell about the time Trigger came in late at a concert in Melbourne?

No, I don't think you did. Just tell me about the sixth raffle. I'll settle for that.

But I got to tell yer how witty Trigger was—to build up his character, as the saying goes. He's late for this concert and the singer on the stage stops warbling and says sarcastic like: "The gentleman with the bald head is late." Quick as a flash, without thinking, Trigger answered him: "You can go and get fixed—for mine." He was witty all right, was old Trigger.

I can see that. . . .

Anyhow, where was I? Ah, yes, up to where Danny O'Connell the publican had a shot at Trigger about the raffle. (You keep interrupting me and I lose track.) O'Connell didn't like raffles being run in his pub on account his customers had only so much money to spend and he liked them to spend it on beer and bets with the SP bookie in the bar who O'Connell financed, see. So he says to Trigger: "Some of my customers are complaining. They say Greenfingers Stratton won your raffle five weeks in a row." Trigger had a good answer as usual. He said: "Old Greenfingers was always lucky." "Yeh," O'Connell replied, "and he's working with a very lucky partner too, if you ask me." "No one asked you, as it turns out," Trigger told him, "but at least we haven't watered that pumpkin and put a collar on it like you do with your beer." You couldn't beat old Trigger in an argument and that's for sure. Anyway, in spite of some bad publicity, they sold six books of tickets. Then, just when Trigger was going to draw Greenfingers' ticket out of the tin, Danny O'Connell said: "Just a minute, I'll draw the raffle this week." Well you can imagine how Trigger felt. He loses all his capital if someone wins that pumpkin off him. So he says: "I don't like no aspersions being cast on my character, but you can draw it, if you insist." And he was thinking fast. "You can draw it at five to six."

What difference did it make when he drew it?

A lot of difference. Trigger calls Greenfingers aside. "Here," he says, "here's six more raffle books. Go and lock yourself in the dunny and fill out every ticket in my name."

So old Trigger won the sixth raffle himself?

As a matter of fact, a bloke named Sniffy Connors won the raffle with the only ticket he ever bought in his life. Greenfingers got writer's cramp filling in six hundred butts. Trigger had half of the tickets but, as luck would have it, O'Connell drew out the one Sniffy Connors bought.

And what did Sniffy do with the pumpkin? Eat it?

Sniffy was living in a tent at the time, so he blew a hole in the side of the pumpkin with a stick of gelignite and made a house out of it. Lived in it for six years with his wife and six kids. . . . I could take you to the spot and show you the house except he got burnt out in the bushfires in 1936.

You win. Have another beer.

Not me. I'm busy today. Running a raffle. The biggest turkey ever bred in Australia. Two bob a time. How many tickets do you want?

12

The Greatest Slanter in the History
of the Racing Game

(as told by Billy Borker in the
Hotel Warrnambool, Warrnambool)

D ID I ever tell you about the time Harry Fenton
and Sam Smith rigged the hurdle race in the
Western District?

No, I don't think you did. Have another beer and
tell me about it.

Thanks. Well, my father knew Harry Fenton and
Sam Smith—knew 'em well. Went to school with Harry,
that's if Harry went to school—which is doubtful. Harry
was a horse-trainer—won a National Steeplechase with
a big bay horse fifty years ago. Later on he got old
and silly, in a way. Used to go round in three shirts and
four overcoats.

You don't say.

Positive fact, so my old man reckoned—wore trousers,
too, of course. Frightened of getting sick, he was.
Frightened of nothing else, though. Had a very lean
time late in life. Melbourne horses kept coming down,
winning the big races. Took to pinching a bit of hay
and running up bills. The other fella, Sam Smith, was
an ex-jockey, very religious—won a race at Flemington

on protest one time, then got smashed up in a fall and took a job cleaning out Harry Fenton's stables. Dirty job, but clean money—that's when Harry had any money, which was rarely. The few horses Harry had lost race after race, year after year—not worth feeding even with someone else's hay. Sam prayed and Harry swore—but it made no difference.

Maybe so, but what about the race they tried to rig?

Coming to that—got to tell the story properly, like my father. As I said, bad trot—never won a race for years. Harry swearing in four overcoats, and Sam praying and sweeping up manure. Debts everywhere. One horse left. Pinching feed for it from a big squatter, name of Urquhart. Season finished, Harry finished, Sam finished. Only one meeting left—country meeting. Horse called The Mercury—very fast, but couldn't jump. Entered him in the hurdle race at this meeting. Good thing if he stands up. But couldn't jump a Toorak front gate.

Have another drink. Why didn't they enter him in a flat race?

Coming to that. Be odds on in a flat race at a country meeting. Three hundred quid in debt. Long price only hope. Entered him in the hurdle, eight to one—'cause he couldn't jump. Harry borrowed a hundred quid from a saddler name of Evans—with The Mercury as security.

Not much good putting a hundred pounds on a horse that couldn't jump.

Old Harry had a scheme, see. Took a trip out to the course the night before the races, with Sam and a hacksaw. Hot night, the moon watching. Harry in his overcoat whistling "The Wild Colonial Boy"; Sam shivering with fright and praying. Out at the course, Harry

71

took the saw and left Sam to mind the jinker. Harry sawing the rails of each hurdle almost through, and Sam waiting in the jinker praying. Sam listened to the saw squawking. Thought it was saying, "We'll go to jail. We'll go to jail. We'll go to jail." He was shivering and sweating at the same time. Harry sawed all the fences. Sawed every rail almost through, so's The Mercury wouldn't fall. Eight to one, the bookies laid. Eight to one 'cause he couldn't jump, and there was no hurdles. Greatest slanter in the history of the racing game, my old man reckoned. Harry put the whole hundred quid on at eight to one.

Cleaned up eight hundred quid on a rigged race, eh?

Matter of fact, The Mercury fell on the flat before they reached the first hurdle. Harry gave up training after that and went on the pension. Sam got religious mania and went into an institution. Not much difference between being on a pension and being in an institution, when you come to think of it. Speaking of the pension. Did I ever tell you about the old age pensioner who cleaned up three policemen during the shearers' strike?

Sorry, I've got to be going now. You can tell me that one tomorrow.

Won't be here tomorrow. I've got a horse running in the hurdle at Colac.

13

The Maoris are Ahead of the Yanks and Russians

(as told by Billy Borker in the
Lygon Hotel, Melbourne)

I SEE by the paper the Russians are going to put another woman into outer space.

You know who put the first woman into outer space?

The Russians, of course. Tereshkova was her name.

That's just where you're wrong. The Maoris did.

Ah, come off it. Another one of your stories, I guess.

No, not mine.

Your father's then.

For once, no. This story was told by a Maori named Te Kore, who was chairman of the Kootimana District Maori Council.

You don't tell.

It was him and no one else. The New Zealand Governor-General, Sir What's-his-name, came to Kootimana to open the meeting-house at the pa.

Pa?

Maori for village. This Governor-General started talking about modern science and Te Kore chipped in and he says: "See that carved figure there of a man and

"Te Kore chipped in . . . !"

a woman, surmounted by a bird. Well, that man is Ueoneone and the woman is his wife, Reitu. Ueoneone, before he was married, had a vision in which he saw a beautiful woman bathing by a waterfall. He took a fancy to this sheila, see"—a'course, I'm not using the Maori's exact words, they don't call women sheilas, naturally; matter of fact the Kiwi calls his wife a dragon for some reason—"so this Maori Ueoneone, back in the olden days, calls on his spirit which was a kokako bird, to go and find this beautiful sheila. Well, the bird flies off right out into orbit and eventually brings back the sheila whose name was Reitu and Ueoneone married her on the spot. So," Te Kore tells the Governor-General, "the Maoris were the first to send a woman into outer space."

Must have been a character this Te Kore. How did you come to know him?

Some of my best friends are Maoris, mate. They're a great people. No fools, either, innocent in the best sense of the word, but not simple. Have all the time in the world. Call the white man a Pakeha, I dunno why. Anyway, this Governor-General character carries on about modern science, atomic submarines and all that, and old Te Kore chips in again, polite and smiling but, like the Maoris usually are, and he says: "The Pakeha should study the ancient history of the Maori people more closely, Your Excellency. Our ancestors came from the land of Hawaiki, which is far across the seas. How did they get to New Zealand? They had no canoes. The first Maori to land here called on a whale named Tohora to help him. He got on the whale's back and the whale swam under the sea to New Zealand. So you see, the Maori was the first to travel under the sea."

Well, by this time, the Governor-General was getting a bit fed up but he carried on regardless, talking about the race to be first to the moon between the Yanks and the Russians. Reckoned he was on pretty safe ground there I suppose. But old Te Kore chips in again with a cheeky but polite grin—and he says. . . .

Don't see how a grin could be cheeky but polite at the same time.

Easy, seeing you don't know some of my Maori mates. That reminds me of the time the Inspector from the New Zealand Social Security Department visited the Maori pa to check up on child endowment. You see, the Maori has a different attitude to possessions than we have; he shares everything with his friends and relations—including his children. It's a positive fact. If one Maori has a lot of children he'll kind of lend some to his mates or relations. Trouble was, in this case I'm telling you about, they claimed child endowment twice for a lot of these kids. See, the real parents and the foster parents each claimed child endowment for the kiddies. So down comes this Inspector. There's only about a hundred children in the pa but about two hundred are being claimed for. He talks to each family separately and counts the children, but he can't tell the little Maori kids apart so, after a while, he gave the game away.

What's this got to do with the argument about the race to the moon?

Ah, I nearly forgot. That's right, Te Kore says to the Governor-General: "Do you know what will happen when the Russians or the Americans get to the moon? There'll be a sign there: PAKEHA GO HOME."

A beauty. He must have been a character this Te Kore.

Was he ever. "The Pakeha will find a Maori woman on the moon by the name of Rona," he says. "Now, the reason Rona is on the moon is that she was real good at cursing and swearing. One night she went out to get a calabash full of water"—a calabash is a dried gourd, a sort of Maori pumpkin, used for carrying water in the olden days. "She was on her way to the spring," old Te Kore says, "when the moon went behind a cloud and caused her to stumble and stub her toe. So she cursed and swore at the moon. And the moon did the lolly"—I slipped into the Australian language again there for a minute. "The moon got annoyed," Te Kore says, "and it reached down and grabbed Rona by the scruff of her neck and lifted her up. As she went she grabbed a tree but that didn't save her because the moon pulled it up by the roots. And," says Te Kore to the Governor-General, "if you look at the moon you can see them, Rona, the calabash, and the tree."

And what did the Governor-General say to that?

What could he say to such a polite man as Te Kore? But if you ask the opinion of Billy Borker, my own personal opinion, the Pakeha will find a Maori tangi going on when they get to the moon.

A tangi?

A tangi is a kind of long funeral, like an Irish wake. Every relative and most friends of the family turn up from all over the country. It just wouldn't occur to a Maori not to go to the tangi of a relative. The body lies in state and they weep and pray, then they eat and drink and sing and dance.

How long for?

77

Some go on for weeks. More man hours lost through tangis than strikes or sickness in New Zealand—so the Government brought in a six-day limit on a tangi.

A very interesting custom, the tangi.

I'll say it is. The Maoris are very civilised people. They have great respect for the dead. Oh, I nearly forgot. You know what old Te Kore says finally to the Governor-General?

Nothing would surprise me.

He says: "So, Your Excellency, the Pakeha will have to consult the Maori before they can reach the moon." "And why is that?" the Governor-General asks. "They'll have to ask the Maoris what Rona said when she swore at the moon," Te Kore tells him.

Not bad, not bad at all. A bit different to your usual yarn.

It's not my yarn, it's Te Kore's.

Does he really exist?

Just go any time to the Kootimana District Council and you'll find him there. The stories he told the Governor-General were old Maori legends. But it was clever how he linked them up with modern science. A'course, he can tell them better than me—a very cultured man is old Te Kore.

14

Australians are the Most Wonderful People in All the World

(as told by Billy Borker in the Mount Druitt Inn, Mount Druitt)

Dᴵᴰ I ever tell you about the Irish migrant who went back to Dublin?

No, I don't think you did. Have a drink and tell me about him. Some migrants who go back to the old country haven't got a good word to say for Australia.

Well, this particular Irishman was different. When he arrived back in Dublin his mate said to him: "And how was it, Pat, old mate, what koind of people are these Aussies after all?" "The Australians?" says Pat—I'll imitate the Irish lingo—"Oi'm glad you asked that question. They're the most wonderful people in all the woide world. And that's the simple truth. With the Australians it's a case of share and share aloike, one for all and all for one. It's what they call mateship. The stranger comes to them and they make him welcome the loike of the prodigal son returning in the Bible and him not a son at all nor any relative even. But the Australians will give him first place by the fire. And, Oi tell yer no loie, if you have no money and the Aussie has two pound, he'll give you one and never ask for it back. Ah, they're darlin' people, the only true Christians left in the world. If you're a fugitive on the run, the Aussie will hoide you and keep you safe. No matter what you do, your Australian mate will defend you. 'A mate can do no wrong.' And no matter who you are, the Australian will give you a fair go."

Here's your beer. He was certainly wrapped up in Australians.

Was he ever.

And there's a lot in what he says.

You admit Aussies are good people, I see. You know, Australians like to be praised. "What do you think of Australia?" that's the first thing they ask a foreign visitor. One time, a Sydney taxi driver asked one of those visiting Yankee wrestlers: "What do you think of Sydney?" And the Yank replies: "I like it—and the thing I like most about it, is there's a daily plane service, so I can get to hell out of this place and go back to God's own country."

Ah, these Yanks think there's no place like the U.S.A. But this Irishman must have met some real nice people while he was here.

Must he ever. Wait till I tell you. So his mate says, "Pat," he says, "they must be marvellous people, the Australians, and no mistake." And Pat is just getting warmed up. "It's loike I'm tellin' yer, they're the most wonderful people in all the world. Let me take just another small example. You know how I loike a drop of the roight stuff? Well, more than once in Australia, Oi took one over the noine and woke up with a mother and a father of a hangover. But, when you've got a hangover, the Aussie, may God bless his endeavours, would offer you a drink to loiven you up. What he calls the hair of the dog that bit you. Ah, they're darlin' boys, people after me own heart. Do you know, if you have no home the Australian will invoite you in to live in his home. And if you have no bed, he'll let you have his bed. And, may God stroike me dead if I tell a loie, if you have no wife, the Australian will let you share his wife."

He could see nothing but good in Australians.

Well, his mate says to him, "Pat," he says. "Oi'll admit from what you say Australians must be foine upstandin' people—but surely you found something in Australia you didn't loike?" Pat hesitates for a moment, rubs his chin and says thoughtfully: "Well, Oi will admit Oi didn't get on too well with the whoite people out there."

I don't believe a word of it.

It's gospel truth. Rolf Harris told it in his show at the Chevron.

15

The Great Australian Larrikin

(as told by Billy Borker in the
Albion Hotel, Parramatta)

WHAT would be the best Australian story you
ever heard, Billy?

The Great Australian Larrikin, as my father
called it, is one of the best, I'd reckon, Jerome.

Have another drink and tell me about him.

Don't mind if I do. This fella's name was Dooley
Franks. A real knockabout man. Lived here in Parramatta. Ran a double, did a bit of urging at the races,
sold smuggled transistors. One night he went to
Tommo's two-up school and won five hundred quid
backing the tail. So he decided to join the Tattersall's
Club. Up he choofs to the uniformed flunkey at the
club door, wearing a polo neck jumper, suede shoes,
and one of them small brimmed hats with a yellow
feather in it. "Here, fill in this form," the flunkey says
dubiously; "the committee will consider your applica-
tion and let you know in due course." When the committee meets, the secretary says: "This Dooley Franks
is an urger. We can't have him in the club." The committee members could not have agreed more: most of
them *used* to be urgers, see. "Dooley Franks hasn't got
two pennies to clink together. Just tell him the joining
fee—a hundred pounds—and that'll be the end of it."

"The committee got really worried!"

So they write Dooley a letter and he bounces back and slams a bundle of tenners on the counter in front of the flunkey. Well, the committee got really worried. The secretary says: "Tell him he has to have three sponsors, famous people, not Australians. The furthest he's ever been from Parramatta is to the Kembla Grange racecourse." They think they've got old Dooley Franks beat, see. So the flunkey tells him: "Three famous people, not Australians." "Why didn't you say so in the first place?" Dooley says, "would have saved time and trouble. Eisenhower (he was President at that time), Khrushchev and the Pope. Just tell 'em Dooley Franks from Parramatta wants a reference."

He was joking, of course?

Wait till I tell yer. Don't spoil the story, mate, one of the best Australian stories every told. Well, the committee got a shock, needless to say. Now, the secretary was a hard case, so he says: "Listen, this here Dooley Franks couldn't know Eisenhower, Khrushchev or the Pope. Tell you what we'll do. We'll offer to take him over to Washington, Moscow and Rome, in person. Then we'll hear no more about it." They write to Dooley Franks and he says: "All right with me. Air letters would be cheaper, but if you insist." The secretary says: "We're stuck with it now. We'll put in a hundred quid each and I'll go with him. It'll be the joke of the century." Away they go by air to Washington, up the steps to the White House. They wait around in corridors for about three days and eventually they get an appointment with one of Eisenhower's side-kicks. "I'm from Tattersall's Club, Sydney," the secretary says. The Yank is puzzled. "Sydney?" he asks, "where's that?" "Australia," the secretary tells him.

"Ah, yeah," the Yank replies. "That's where we sell all our old films to the television stations." "We want to see President Eisenhower," the secretary says. "You can't just come here and see the President. You have to have an appointment." Well, Dooley Franks is getting a bit impatient, see, so he says: "Listen, just tell Ike Dooley Franks wants to see him. The bloke who pinched six tins of petrol for him when his car ran out on the road to Paris. Dooley Franks from Parramatta." Well, the Yank goes away and comes back. "Mister Franks," he says, "why didn't you say so in the first place? President Eisenhower will see you right away." "Can I come too?" the secretary says. "No, the President wants to have a private chat with Mister Franks."

Surely he didn't actually know Eisenhower?

Well, he came back six hours later high as a kite. "Sorry to keep you waiting," he tells the secretary. "Me and Ike got talking old times over a few drinks and lost track of time." So they head off for Moscow.

Ah, don't tell me . . .

Up to the Kremlin gates with an interpreter they go. Freezing cold night, thirty-eight below. The secretary puts over a spiel about the Tattersall's Club and Dooley tells the bloke on the gate: "Just tell Nikita that Dooley Franks from Parramatta wants to see him. Was treasurer of the Sheepskins For Russia appeal during the war, sailed on the North Sea convoys and sold Russian magazines on the Sydney waterfront." Well, to make a long story short, the same thing happens: Khrushchev wants to see Comrade Franks, and the secretary of the Tattersall's Club is left freezing in the Red Square. Dooley comes out eventually, and next day they head for Rome. And the secretary is thinking: What will I tell the committee when I get back? They'll never believe me. If he gets in to see the Pope, I'm going with him.

And did he?

Well, they see a cardinal, but he says you have to make an appointment for an audience with the Pope. So Dooley tells him: "Just say Dooley Franks from Parramatta; was an altar boy at St Patrick's Cathedral, got a brother a priest and a sister a nun." The cardinal comes back—if you don't believe me you can ask old Dooley himself—he says the Pope will grant a private audience to Mister Franks. The secretary begs to be let in. "I must see them together," he says. "His Holiness wishes to see only Mister Franks. But if you want to see them together you can stand down in the square. His Holiness will appear on the balcony at one o'clock and I'll arrange for Mister Franks to stand with him." Well, the secretary is desperate: what's he going to tell the committee? He goes away and comes back at one o'clock. The square is packed with fifty thousand people. The secretary is so far away he can't even see the balcony. The crowd cheers. There's a Yankee tourist standing near by with a pair of field-glasses. The secretary begs him: "Lend me your field-glasses." The Yank says: "They're not field-glasses, they're binoculars. And you can't borrow them. I've come ten thousand miles to see the Vatican. . . ." The secretary says: "Well, what can you see?" "Two men standing on the balcony," the Yank tells him. The secretary tugs his arm. "Can you recognise them? Who are they?" The Yank takes a good look through his binoculars: "Well, I can't place the guy in the funny hat but the other guy is definitely Dooley Franks from Parramatta."

Now I've heard everything.

16

The World's Worst Worrier

(as told by Billy Borker in the
Oxford Hotel, Darlinghurst)

You know you ought to write your stories down,
Billy.

Written stories are no good, all made up. My
stories are true.

But if you wrote them down you might become a
famous author.

Australian writers do no good in Australia. No man
can be a rabbi in his own village, as the saying goes. But
I did remember another story. The world's worst
worrier, it's called.

Sounds good. Have a drink and tell me about it.

Well, there was this fella who couldn't stop worrying. He worked overtime at it. The lowest paid clerk
in the biggest office in Martin Place. Worried when he
couldn't balance the stamp money; worried when it
balanced, because he must have made a mistake. Worried
he might get the sack; worried he might get into a rut
if he stayed in the job too long. Worried when he
didn't have a TV set; then bought one on the never-
never and worried about meeting the payments. Worried
because he had no children; then worried that he might
have children and not be able to bring them up right.

Worried that his wife might be unfaithful to him; and worried that she must be a dull woman when other men took no interest in her. Worried because he thought people were talking about him; and worried because people weren't interested in him.

Must have been a worrier all right.

Was he ever. The world's worst, like I told you. Had an anxiety complex so big that Winterset couldn't have jumped over it.

If he ever stopped worrying, he worried because he had nothing to worry about. It got so bad his wife started worrying because he was worried; and he started worrying about his wife being worried. Then he started worrying about the Hydrogen Bomb—and that really sent him around the bend. So he went to one of those psychiatrists.

There's a lot of mental illness about.

It's the Bomb, mate, and the stress of the rat race to make money. They're all mad except you and me, mate, and you strike me as a bit queer at times.

Thank you. Did the psychiatrist do him any good?

No good at all. Made him worse, in fact. He started worrying about how he'd pay the psychiatrist's bills. Anyway, he went from bad to worse until the psychiatrist decided he'd have to go to the Looney bin. Then a funny thing happened. At work, he had a share in a jackpot lottery ticket. Used to worry about not being able to afford it but didn't pull out because he was worried what the others would say. Then, strike me dead if I tell a lie, his syndicate won the big prize. His share was ten thousand lovely quid.

Well, at last he could stop worrying.

Not him, he started to worry what to do with the

money. Lay awake at night thinking people would touch him for it. Well, one day one of his mates at work, a bit of a hard case, said: "What are you worrying about? You've got plenty of money: why don't you employ someone to do your worrying for you?" So he puts an advert in the paper. WORRIER REQUIRED. ONLY EXPERIENCED MEN NEED APPLY. EXCELLENT SALARY.

Now just a minute . . .

Gospel truth, mate. Not only did he put the ad. in but he got a reply. A little skinny fella with worry lines all over his face and haunted eyes. Had good references, too. Been bankrupt twice. Married twice and both his wives left him, which worried him a lot for some reason. A bigger worrier than his new employer, if that was possible. Of course, the world's worst worrier had to make sure he had the right man. Was going to pay big money. He asked him a lot of questions—but he couldn't fault him. At last he asked: "Do you bite your fingernails, like me?" And the applicant replied: "I'm such a worrier, I bite other people's fingernails." Well that clinched it. He gave him the job and stopped worrying on the spot.

And I suppose he and his wife lived happily ever after.

They went for a trip to the Barrier Reef. He never worried. Always bright and cheerful. Stopped biting his fingernails. Made his wife the happiest woman in Australia. If he got a worry he just referred it to the professional worrier. The most happy-go-lucky man in the world, he became.

Well, at least, that story has a happy ending.

One day his wife said to him: "I hate to worry you

89

dear, but because you are paying that man so much
to do your worrying, all your money has gone and
you're in debt."

And what did he say to that?

"No good you coming to me," he said, "that's *his*
worry."

17

A Shaggy Billiard Table Story

(as told by Billy Borker in the
Sundowner Hotel, Punchbowl)

Do you know any of these new elephant stories?
No. Got up for gigs. Don't see any point in
them.

What about shaggy dog stories?

No, they were just a passing fad. I stick to facts,
mate, only tell true stories. I did hear a shaggy billiard
table story once, though.

A shaggy billiard table story. That's something
new. . . .

Nothing new under the sun.

Have a drink and tell me about it.

Don't mind if I do. Set 'em up again, Fred. There
was this millionaire went into a billiard table manufac-
turer's factory and said he wanted to buy a table. "We
have an excellent range, sir," the salesman said. "I want
a table made to my own specifications," says the millionaire. Well, the salesman gets out his pen and notebook.
"You just give me the specifications, sir, and we'll do
the rest." "Ordinary billiard tables haxe six legs on them,
right?" the millionaire says. "Right, sir," the salesman
says, working on the time-honoured idea that the
customer is always right, "I can see you know your

billiard tables, sir." "Well, my table must have only one leg in the middle," the millionaire tells him. The salesman starts to write it down. Then he hesitates: "Only one leg, sir?" "Only one," the millionaire tells him again. "That's what I thought you said, sir. Did you have any other special features in mind, sir?" "Well, I did, as a matter of fact," the millionaire says. "The ordinary common run of billiard table has green baize cloth, right?" "How right you are, sir," the salesman says. "Well, my table must have mink fur cloth instead."

A bit unusual you telling a story about a millionaire, isn't it? You generally tell them about seamen or taxi drivers or . . .

Or raffle kings. Well this isn't really one of my father's stories. You said you wanted a shaggy dog story and, seeing as I don't go in for them I'm telling you a shaggy billiard table story instead.

It sounds like a shaggy billiard table and no mistake.

Well, the salesman eyes this millionaire off, see. He must be pulling my leg surely, he thinks. "Mink cloth, sir? Did you say mink cloth?" "I did indeed," the millionaire says. The salesman writes it down and says, "There wouldn't be any other special features, would there, sir?" "The ordinary common or garden billiard table has rubber cushions, right?" What's he coming at now? the salesman thinks. "Well, my table must have gold-plated cushions." The salesman writes it down thinking, this bloke's as queer as a three pound note, hasn't got all his marbles, so he says sarcastically: "Will that be all now? Sure there isn't some other little feature we can put on it for you?"

Beyond a joke, I should say.

The salesman puts his notebook away. "There's just one other thing," the millionaire says. "Pool room billiard tables have six pockets, right?" "Yeh, they have six pockets, but we're very busy today. . . ." "Well," the millionaire tells him, "my table must have only one pocket, right in the middle, three feet in diameter."

Must have been a keen billiard player that millionaire. He was real keen, as it turned out. Anyway, the salesman goes into the manager's office and he says: "There's a ratbag out there wants a special billiard table made with one leg, mink cloth, gold-plated cushions and only one hole three feet in diameter right in the middle." "You're joking, of course," the manager replied. "I'm not but I think he is," the salesman says, "what will I tell him?" The manager thinks it over and he says: "The first of April today. It's an April Fool's Day joke. Tell him we'll make the table with great pleasure but it will cost a hundred thousand pounds."

The salesman goes out and tells this bloke the table will cost him a hundred thousand nicker. But the millionaire doesn't turn a hair. "I'll write you out a cheque right away," he says, "but there's just one other thing. It must be finished in three weeks, and installed when I come back from my honeymoon. I'm going in my yacht to Surfers' Paradise." Well, the salesman takes the cheque and scarpers back into the manager's office. "He's given me a cheque," he tells the manager, "and wants the table finished in three weeks." The manager says, "He's a cheeky mug. A joke's a joke, but this is going too far." So he gets on the phone to the millionaire's bank—and—do you know what?—it turned out that the cheque was fair dinkum. "Why not make the table?" says the manager. "For a hundred thousand he can have all the special features he wants and a year's supply of chalk chucked in." Paid a hundred thousand fiddleydids for a billiard table. More money than sense, some of these silvertails.

He really was a millionaire, after all?

One of the uppity upper bracket, mate, and a keen billiardist, into the bargain.

Must have been to play on a table like that.

Well, away he choofs on his honeymoon to Surfers' Paradise in his luxury yacht. And he lies in the sun with his beautiful young bride while the tradesmen knock together this special billiard table.

That's the way of the world.

Yeh, and on his way back, the yacht ran into a great storm and it sunk. Lost all hands.

You're pulling my leg again. Whew, look at the time. I've got to be going.

Hooroo. If you hear of anyone who wants a good billiard table I know where they can get one cheap.

18

The Taxi Driver who Sat on the Central Station Rank for Three Days and Nights

(as told by Billy Borker in the
Railway Hotel, Parramatta)

Did I ever tell about the taxi driver who sat on the
Central Station rank, Sydney, for three days
and nights during the Depression?

No, I don't think you did. Have a drink and tell me
about him.

Don't mind if I do. Well, things were real bad in
the cab game in those days, needless to say. These young
fellas who drive taxis now don't know they're alive, I
can tell you. Cabs on the prowl everywhere then and
no fares. People use to hide behind a telephone post
when they hailed a cab in those days.

What was the purpose of doing that?

Well, the cabs would come up on the footpath after
you.

You don't tell.

If you don't believe me, you can ask old Hungry
Hanrahan. He's been driving Sandy McNabs for thirty-
five years, so he ought to know.

I guess he would.

You can say that again. The greatest potsitter, mul-

95

tiple loader and fare fleecer that ever sat behind a steering wheel, was old Hungry. Drove an orange-guard taxi in Sydney during the Depression, needless to say. You know what he did one time. He drove a fella to Glebe. A three bob fare according to Hungry's meter. The fare refused to pay. Said another taxi company had driven him there for one and sixpence. So he demanded that Hungry take him to the police station. Well, Hungry obliged—without switching the meter off, of course. At the Bastille the lollipop said the fare must pay the price showing on the meter. "The least you can do is take me home again," the fella in the cab said. Hungry did the right thing; took him home. And when they got there the meter was showing seven and six.

What's that got to do with the bloke who . . . what did he do again?

Sat on the Central rank for three days and nights. But before you can appreciate the story you've got to under-stand how things were in the cab game during the Depression.

I can imagine it. Get on with your story.

Another thing you've got to realise is that taxi drivers weren't born thieves, they become thieves after they started to drive taxis—because of the terms of employment.

Oh, I don't know. Some of my best friends are taxi drivers.

I suppose you'd know better than me. I knew a cab driver once who drove his mother-in-law to the hospital to die and charged her full fare.

Get on with your story.

You always interrupt just when I'm getting started.

In those days, the line of cabs on Central Station rank extended out into Elizabeth Street, down Hunter Street to Castlereagh Street, then down the hill to Circular Quay. There was a telephone at the front of the rank and sometimes a shrewdie on the rear of the queue would ring up and send the front cab off on a wild goose chase. And if you left your cab to have a feed or a sleep, other drivers would shift it out of the queue to the other side of the road. So this bloke I'm telling you about, Hungry Hanrahan, took no risks: he slept in the cab and his wife brought him sandwiches and tea at mealtimes—not a bad drop of beer this—well, at last he got to the front of the queue. And eventually, a big fella came out of the station. A squatter from the bush by the look of him: wide-brimmed hat, old-fashioned clothes, and kept looking around at the tall buildings. Needless to say, Hungry couldn't get out and get his claws on the squatter's luggage quick enough. "The Australia Hotel," the man from back o' Bourke said after he got in the back seat. You wouldn't read about it, would you, waited three days and nights then got a fare to the Australia Hotel, about half a mile away.

Don't see much point in the story. Not up to your usual standard.

Wait till I tell you. He slewed on to this bloke in the back, looking around with his mouth open and his eyes sticking out so you would have knocked them off with a stick, and he asked him: "New to Sydney are you, mate?" "Yes," replied the squatter, "first time I've been down. It's a big place, isn't it?"

Don't tell me this is one of those corny stories where someone sells a squatter the Town Hall or the clock over the gents in Martin Place.

"A squatter from back o' Bourke by the look of him . . . !"

There you go again, trying to tell the story for me. This cab driver was a quick thinker—but. . . . "I've been recommended to the Australia Hotel," the squatter said. "And that's where I'll take you," Hungry Hanrahan said. And he put the flag down and drove off down Parramatta Road.

But that's not the way to the Australia Hotel from Central Station.

My father always said . . .

Never mind your father.

Anyway, he took the squatter all the way to Parramatta, then across country to Ryde, through Pymble and along the Pacific Highway back to Sydney. The meter was showing five quid when they eventually pulled up outside the Australia Hotel.

And did the squatter pay up?

When the cab pulled up, the squatter said: "I don't doubt the Australia is a good hotel, but it's too far out of the city. I'd have to do too much travelling. Could you recommend me to a good hotel in the heart of the city?"

The plot thickens.

It's like I told you. All cab drivers are thieves. Of course, they weren't born thieves; it's what you call an occupational disease. So he drove the squatter back along the Pacific Highway through Pymble and Ryde to Parramatta, then along Parramatta Road to Sydney —and he dropped him at the Carlton Hotel right opposite the Australia. Ten quid—the biggest taxi fare ever paid in Australia until that Yank took a cab to Mount Isa.

You're a bigger liar than Tom Pepper.

What? That's lovely that is! If you don't believe

me you can ask old Hungry Hanrahan. Still driving cabs at seventy, is old Hungry. No pensions for cab drivers, you know, and no sick or holiday pay. They just drive until they drop dead at the wheel. Did I ever tell you about the time old Hungry took a bloke to the Menangle Trots and got lost?

No, I don't think you did, but I must go now.

Pity, that. One of the best stories I ever heard—and I'm still thirsty.

You can tell me some other time. I'm late for an important appointment at the Australia Hotel.

I'm your man. My cab's parked outside—I'm driving a shift for Hungry Hanrahan. Hop in and I'll have you at the Australia in next to no time. By the way, how well do you know Sydney?

19

Everyone Reads the Signs They Want to See

(as told by Billy Borker in
the Sefton Hotel, Sefton)

Dᴵᴰ I ever tell you about the death of Murphy the bookmaker.

No, I don't think you did. Have another drink and tell me about it.

Don't mind if I do. Funny thing. I was going to go fishing this morning so I watched the weather forecast last night on the TV, see. Anyway, the weather man points his stick at the wiggley lines on the map and he says: "Rain. Squally southerly winds, heavy seas." I looks at the sign and I says to meself: "He's all up the pole. A low pressure there and a high here. It'll be fine, light winds, seas slight." So I set the alarm for daylight—but the weather man was right for once: howling wind, and raining cats and dogs.

What's all this got to do with Murphy the bookmaker?

A lot to do with him. The moral of the story is that everyone reads the signs they want to see. A parson sees a text from the Bible, a socialist a text from Karl Marx—a fisherman sees signs of fine weather.

Here's your beer. Get on with the story.

Well, there were these two unemployed fellows during the Depression, see. They used to hang around this pub in Footscray. Mad punters, they were, that's when they had any money, which was seldom in those days.

What about Murphy the bookmaker?

You're trying to make me get ahead of the story again. My father always said . . .

Never mind your father. . . .

Ah, not a bad drop of beer that—never touched the sides.

Well, have another and get to the point.

Thanks, well, these two punters' names were Ticktacker Tom and Ron the Runner.

And what have these crazy nicknames got to do with the story?

A lot to do with it. All nicknames have a meaning.

Here's your beer. What about Murphy?

I'll force another one down, just to be sociable. You see, Murphy started his illustrious career as the SP bookmaker in this very pub. And he gave Ticktacker Tom and Ron the Runner a bit of work helping him to take the bets of a Saturday. Murphy would take sixpenny bets or threepence each way and Tom and Ron would go around Footscray collecting bets off old sheilas and battlers.

How did they come to get such fantastic nicknames?

Who? Ticktacker Tom and Ron the Runner? Well, Murphy was a good bookmaker. Gave a bit of credit during a bad trot and always settled on the knocker. Very popular fella in Footscray was Murphy, very popular. Eventually, he got a licence to make a book on the flat at Flemington racecourse. And he was a pretty shrewd fella, old Spud, so he decided to employ a runner and a ticktacker.

What on earth is a ticktacker, if it's not a rude question?

You don't know what a ticktacker is? Well, I'll tell you. You see, in those days there was no broadcasting system on the racecourses and no tote and most of the bookies had no betting boards. And a bookie could easily get caught laying too long a price about a horse.

I don't get it.

Well. Say Murphy, who's out on the flat in a small way, is laying ten to one about a horse, see, and there's money for it, big money in the paddock. Clear?

Clear as a London fog.

Well, I'll put it another way. Murphy wanted to know what price the big bookies were laying about every horse in the paddock. He wanted to get the drum when a horse was backed, so he could cut its price without laying a bet—that's an old satchel-swinger's custom.

Satchel-swinger?

Forget it. So Ticktacker Tom would be in the paddock, see, and every time a horse was heavily supported and its price fell, he'd rush over to the fence and signal to Ron, who'd be waiting there. Tom would wave his hands around for all the world like a buyer at a wool sale or a priest giving a blessing at a funeral. That's what they call ticktacking. Well, these signs would give the number and the odds of horses. Ron, who could read these signs—couldn't read writing but he could read these signs—would run for his life over to tell Murphy the prices. Hairylegs has shortened to ten to one, Gravy Beef has drifted to twenties, and so on.

Ticktacker Tom and Ron the Runner, eh?

Yeh, that's how they got their names. Anyway, all good things come to an end. Murphy did very well as a course bookie, made a lot of money and eventually he got a licence to operate inside on the rails at all Melbourne racecourses. So he didn't need a ticktacker or a runner any more: he set the prices and took all bets without fear or favour. But he didn't forget his mates when he kicked on. If Ticktacker Tom and Ron were at the races and went broke, they could always have a bet on the nod with Murphy and many a time he slung them a quid when things were crook.

Must have been a good fellow, Murphy?

Was he ever. Educated himself, joined the Tattersall's Club, made a million, married a beautiful woman, had six lovely kids and two big mansions—but he never became a snob. Any Footscray battler could get a few quid off Murphy, just for the asking. Most popular man in Footscray, he was. Ticktacker Tom and Ron the Runner thought the sun shone out of his backside. They were very upset when he died, I can tell you.

Oh, he did die eventually?

Its like I told you, that's what the story's all about. The death of Murphy the bookmaker.

So we're getting to the point at last.

Yeh, but out of respect to the dead we ought to drink to his memory and my glass is empty.

All right, I can take a hint—same again.

Thanks. Well, Murphy was a good-hearted fella, one of those philanthropists. Donated more money to charity than you could poke a stick at. Was very generous to the church, too. So when he died the archbishop himself took the burial service in the cathedral. Anyway,

Ticktacker Tom and Ron the Runner were very broke up about Murphy dying, like I told you, but Ron says: "We can't very well go to the funeral." "Why not?" Tom says. "Well, us with our shabby clothes and down-at-heel shoes, and all them toffs dressed up to the nines. We'd look out of place." But Ticktacker Tom insists: "Doesn't matter; Murphy would expect us to go," he says. Ron the Runner was very fond of Murphy, too; he couldn't read anything but ticktackers' language but he had a heart of gold. So off they go to the funeral service.

This better have a good ending.

Ticktacker Tom and Ron the Runner sneak in, take off their hats, and sit in the back row. They kneel down with heads bowed out of respect for Murphy and to hide their old clothes amongst the toffs. They can see the coffin there. The archbishop comes out and conducts a beautiful ceremony and at the finish, he swishes holy water over Murphy's coffin and gives his blessing. He reads softly in Latin and waves his hand for all the world like a ticktacker on a racecourse. Ticktacker Tom breaks down and starts crying: "I can't believe Murphy's dead," he says to Ron. Ron the Runner is watching the archbishop's hand waving around, reading the signs. "I can't believe he's dead," Ticktacker Tom says again. Ron the Runner was still watching the archbishop making signs. "He's dead, all right," he says. "He's drifted to thirty-threes."

Not bad, an unusual twist.

It's like I said: people read the signs they want to see.

20

The World's Worst Pessimist

(as told by Billy Borker in the
Royal George Hotel, Sydney)

D^{ID} I ever tell you about the World's Worst
Pessimist?

No, I don't think you have. You've told me
about the world's worst worrier. . . .

That's a different bloke altogether. A worrier and
a pessimist are two different kinds of cattle. Funny
thing, that, you wouldn't expect happy-go-lucky people
like Australians to be pessimists, but, brother, when
you strike an Australian pessimist he's the world's worst—
and that's for sure. I was at the races with the greatest
pessimist this side of the black stump. Calamity, the
World's Worst Pessimist, we call him.

Where do you get these nicknames from . . . do all
these blokes really exist?

Calamity, the World's Worst Pessimist, exists all
right. I was at the races on Saturday with him and he
put the kibosh on me.

Have a drink and tell me about him.

Don't mind if I do. A nice drop of beer here and
good company: seamen, beatniks and wharfies, the only
real rebels left, these days. Well we chooff to Royal
Randwick, me and old Calamity. And I've got a hot
tip, see. But Calamity says: "If I back it, it won't win,

I'm too unlucky. It'll get left at the post or fall over if I back it." "Don't mozz a man," I tells him. "You're well named, I'll say that for you, Calamity."

Calamity, eh? I get it. Here's your beer. Did the horse win?

Wait till I tell you. Calamity says: "If it drifts in the market, I won't back it, it'll be dead." Then he says: "If it's too short, I won't back it either. I'm only a battler. Can't afford to take short prices." Well, the horse, Magger was its name, opens at eight to one, then gradually drifts to fifteen to one. "It's not trying," Calamity whinges. "It's an SP job," I tells him, "they'll back it off the course." Anyway I had a tenner on it at twenty to one. Calamity only put two quid on it. And you'd think he was peeling it off his rump, the way he moaned. Two hundred lovely quid for me and forty for Calamity. So he starts working overtime at his pessimism: "I'm too unlucky. It'll get beat. You shouldn't have let me back it. Too big a risk for a battler like me. I'm so unlucky that if it was raining mansions I'd get hit on the head with a Mallee lavatory."

Must have been good company at the races, old Calamity.

Was he ever. Anyway, the horse was trained by an ex-Sixth Divvy digger with a gamee leg who loved his horses better than his missus—would sit up all night if his horse was sick and give it penicillin; if his missus was sick, he'd give her two aspros. "He'll pull Magger up," Calamity moans. "He couldn't lay straight in bed." Anyway, starting time comes and we go up in the stand. "They're off," the roar goes up. "It's got left, dead last," Calamity moans. "Rubbish," I says, "it's lying fourth, on the rails." "Well, it won't win," he yells in me ear, "I'm too unlucky." They turn for home and Magger's lying third on the rails, going easy, head on its chest waiting to pounce on the leaders. "It's pocketed on the rails," Calamity yells, "it can't get through." Just as he spoke, the leaders swung wide and Magger goes through along the paint and dashes three lengths clear. "It's home!" I yelled, "what price Magger!" With that, Calamity jumped on me back, shouting: "It'll fall over and break its neck. I'm too unlucky." I stagger down the steps under his weight. Magger is four lengths in front at the leger. Last thing I see as I collapse under Calamity's weight, is a horse flying on the outside, Red Wind, the favourite, but it's too late, Magger has the race won. And Calamity is yelling, "The favourite's finishing like a rocket. What'd I tell yer?" I struggle to my feet just as they pass the post locked together but I thought Magger had lasted. "Close: but Magger by a head," the course announcer Ken Howard says, "London to a brick on Magger." But Calamity was not convinced. "Ken Howard's never been wrong picking a photo result—but there's always a first time." And sure enough, Howard *was* wrong. Magger got beat by a nose.

Be a long time before you go to the races with Calamity again, I'll bet?

You can say that again. But that's not the real story of Calamity. That's just an example of the kind of bloke he is.

Well, have another beer and get on with the real story, for goodness' sake.

Don't mind if I do. Well, the real story of the World's Worst Pessimist is about the time the flash young fella met Calamity on a bus stop and asks him the time. Calamity looks at him, sniffs and says in a whining voice: "You know what will happen if I tell you the time? Well, I'll tell you. We'll get to talking, see, and before we know where we are you'll have missed your last bus." Well, this young bloke can't believe his ears and he says: "Look, I just asked you the time. I haven't got a watch. . . ." Calamity looks at him suspiciously. "You haven't got a watch, eh? How come you haven't got a watch? You're well dressed. You've got a job haven't you?" The young bloke wondered what he'd struck. "I've got a good job. There's no need for us to get talking." "But we are talking aren't we?" Calamity says. "Was that your last bus that just passed? What did I tell you? You've missed your last bus. Now, I'm an hospitable working man. I can't let you sleep in the park or walk home."

Here's your beer. Calamity was well named.

Thanks. Wait till I tell you. Then Calamity says: "Next thing, I'll invite you home to my place. That's the caper, isn't it? And you'll come home. And you'll meet my wife. She's a kind-hearted woman and she'll make up the bed in the spare room so you can sleep at our place. And tomorrow at breakfast I'll introduce you to my daughter who's a sweet innocent kid of eighteen. And you'll take a fancy to her. I know your type, a lady-killer in your pointed shoes and stovepipe trousers and sideboards. Just the type to turn a young girl's head with your slimy cunning ways. Don't argue with me. I know your type, a philanderer from way back. I'm good-hearted, see, gullible, I wouldn't wake up to you see? And you'd end up staying for three months." The young fella tries to get a word in but Calamity is wound up: "And you'd start taking my

BUS STOP
1ᴬ 3 15 18

"*I know your type . . . !*"

daughter out. And me and my wife will lay awake nearly every night, late, worried stiff. And then one day you'll disappear and our poor little daughter will come to us in tears and tell us you've put her in the family way—and left her for dead."

He was a pessimist, all right.

The world's worst, like I told you. But as Bernard Shaw once said, you ain't heard nothing yet. The kid is nearly in tears by now. "Look, I only asked you the time. . . ." Calamity glares at him: "See where a thing like that can lead? You know what I'll do to you when you put my lovely little daughter in the family way? I'll find you, mate, I'll find you, even if you go to the other end of the earth. And I'll have a shot-gun and I'll shoot you stone bloody dead." Calamity grabs him by the shiny lapels of his coat. "And do you know what they'll do to me? They'll find me guilty of murder and put me in jail for the term of me natural life. That's what they'll do to me. I'll end up spending the rest of me life in jail—all because a flash bastard like you is too miserable to buy a watch."

Not bad at all. The world's worst pessimist, eh?

Yeh, Calamity, himself.

Have another drink and tell me something. Did you really know this bloke? Does the World's Worst Pessimist really exist?

Who? Calamity? A'course he exists. Didn't I tell you: I was at the races with him last Saturday.

I wondered why you spoiled the story with that bit at the beginning.

It's like my father always said: "A yarn must not only be true, it must appear to be true." By the way, what time is it?

21

Everybody's Got a Nickname on the Wellington Waterfront

(as told by Billy Borker in the Ship Inn, Sydney)

YOU'RE late today, Billy.

Yeh, I met an old mate of mine from Wellington, New Zealand, Torpedo Joe Coppersmith by name. He's over here having a spell on twenty-five quid and half the cargo in Sydney.

Torpedo Joe. Where would he get a name like that?

I can't rightly say. Everybody's got a nickname on the Wellington waterfront.

How do you know?

How do I know? I worked on the wharves in Wellington years ago, that's how. Great fellas the Wellington wharfies—and they've all got nicknames. One bloke they called the Chief Justice.

Why call a wharfie a Chief Justice?

He was always sitting on a case. Another was called the Reluctant Fish because he wouldn't go near a hook. Great yarn-spinners, the Wellington wharfies. I heard some terrific yarns while I was over there. One was about nicknames as a matter of fact.

Have a beer and tell me about it.

Well, there were these two Wellington wharfies, great mates, one a Kiwi and the other a Maori.

Are there Maoris on the wharves there?

What? About one in four are Maoris. The Maoris and the Kiwis get along well. There's no race prejudice on the Wellington wharves. Did I ever tell you about Hori, the Maori who swallowed the tote ticket?

No, I don't think you did.

Well, I don't intend to. You see if you call a Maori Hori it's just like calling an American negro Sambo, or an Australian aboriginal Jacky. The white man who says it means well, but it's patronising, if you get what I mean.

Here's your beer. Didn't you start off to tell me about the nicknames on the Wellington waterfront?

You keep interrupting. Thanks, not a bad drop here. A bit better than Auckland beer. A Maori asked me: "What do you think of our beer?" "Mate," I tells him, "in Australia we'd use it to poison dingoes." He never turned a hair. "With beer it's what you get used to," he says. Very easy-going fellas, Maoris; so are the Kiwis for that matter. If you criticised beer like that in Sydney or Melbourne, you'd get knocked rotten. Every man likes his own beer. In New Zealand they have these trays like we use for milk bottles and, when it's your shout, you take the glasses up to the bar in one of these trays and get them filled. "Make sure you've got one left for yourself," they used to say to me. And they have these half-gallon jars and they get them filled. Every second bloke you see in Wellington or Auckland is carrying one of those bags usually used for carrying bowls. Some character discovered that these bags would neatly hold two half-gallon flagons. Now the shops do a roaring trade in bowling bags. And they have special plastic stoppers for the flagons.

What's all this got to do with the story you were going to tell me.

This is a New Zealand story and you have to know about the background, the Kiwis and the Maoris and their beer and the waterfront pubs—and nicknames. And this background is dry country. . . .

I can take a hint. Have another drink and get to the point.

The Wellington wharfies drink mainly at two pubs across the road from the wharves, the Waterloo and the Pier. A few drink at the Post Office—the pub, not the real post office, a'course. They drink close by on account of the wind.

What?

The wind. Wellington is called the windy city—by people who come from Auckland—there's a kind of Melbourne-Sydney type rivalry.

The Wellingtonites boast about their airport, only ten minutes to the Town Hall. Aucklandites boast about their harbour bridge, and they don't forget to rub it in about the wind in Wellington. They reckon it's the only city in the world where, if you walk around a block, the cold wind hits you in the face on every corner.

Here's your beer. This story was supposed to be about a Kiwi and a Maori. . . .

So it is—if only you'd stop interrupting—and about everybody having a nickname on the Wellington waterfront. Anyway, there was this Kiwi and his nickname was the Kaiwharawhara Murderer.

The what? How would he get a name like that?

The Kaiwharawhara Murderer? Well, actually, they sometimes called him the Kaiwhara Murderer for short. Anyway he lived at Kaiwharawhara, a suburb of Wellington, and he got his name because he was always saying, "I'll murder that so and so." Every time he got annoyed, he'd say: "I'll murder him." Blokes reckoned it must have been standing room only at the Kaiwharawhara cemetery and that the Murderer was working on commission for a couple of funeral directors. Actually, he was a mild sort of coot who wouldn't harm a fly. His best mate was a Maori—you often see that in New Zealand—white men and coloured as mates, more than you do in Australia. And this Maori was called the Smiling Seagull.

The Smiling Seagull?

Yes. He was a happy-go-lucky cove, always smiling, and he was a casual wharfie at the time I'm telling you about, during the Second World War it was, and they call casuals "seagulls". Anyway, the Kaiwharawhara Murderer and the Smiling Seagull were great mates all their lives. One lunch hour during the war, they head off to the Pier for a few glasses of Red Band. In those days, the wharfies had to have a ticket to get through the gate. War precautions and that kind of thing. This particular day, a Friday it was, there was a new copper on the gate, a keen young Englishman. The Smiling Seagull heads back to work while the Kaiwharawhara Murderer gets his two flagons filled for the weekend. At the gate the young policeman stops the Seagull and he says: "Where's your ticket?" The Seagull smiles a bit wider than usual and searches his pockets. "That's funny. I must have left it in my coat on the wharf." And the copper replies, "Well, you can't come on the wharf without it." The Seagull stops smiling. "But I'm late. All the boys are back at work and I've got to start right away." "Stand aside," the copper says, "you can't come in without a ticket." Pretty soon the old Murderer choofs along. The Seagull starts smiling again. "Here he comes me mate," he says, "he works on the wharf. He'll vouch for me." "Do you know this man," the constable says to the Murderer. "Know him?" says the Murderer. "Known him all me life. He's me best mate." The policeman says, "He hasn't got his ticket. What's his name?" "Name?" the Murderer says. "His *name*?" A blank look comes over his face and he scratches his head. "Jack, er Bill . . . it's ridiculous, I went to school with him. His name is, er . . . the Seagull, the Smiling Seagull.

He couldn't remember his real name?

No, he'd been calling him the Smiling Seagull or Seagull for short for so long he'd forgotten it. Anyway, the constable is determined: "Where's *your* ticket?" he asks the Murderer. Well, the Murderer had left his ticket in his coat on the wharf, too. This really made the policeman suspicious: "You can't get in, either of you. Stand aside. I might have to take you down to the police station." The Seagull stops smiling again. "We gotta get in," he says, "we'll lose our jobs." The constable called the Seagull aside: "You claim this man has known you all his life. What's *his* name?" The Seagull smiles again. "His name?" he says. "*His* name? You're asking me his name. Listen, he's my mate, we come from the same pa. A'course he's not a Maori but he lived next door when we were kids and now we live next door to each other out at Kaiwharawhara."

"Well, just tell me his name." "His *name*? Er, Bill, Tom, er Ernie. . . . Just a minute, it's on the tip of me tongue, know it as well as he knows mine. Aw heck—the Kaiwharawhara Murderer, that's who he is. We call him the Murderer for short."

Didn't know each other's names, eh?

Only the nicknames. Anyway, by this time the young copper is ready to go up the wall—and he's very suspicious: "Why do you call him the Murderer?" The Seagull smiles widely: "Because he's always murdering someone." The policeman gets his book out: "There was a woman murdered at Kaiwharawhara last week." The old Seagull couldn't resist the joke at his mate's expense. "Ah, me mate would have killed her, he's got a private cemetery out there." The policeman says sternly: "I'm afraid you two will have to accompany me to the station and I must warn you that anything you say will be taken down and may be used in evidence." On the way to the police station they meet the Chief Timekeeper. The Murderer is real worried by this time: "Here's the Chief Timekeeper. He knows us. He'll vouch for us." So the copper says to this timekeeper: "Do you know these two men?" "Know 'em?" the timekeeper says. "A'course I know 'em, the two greatest loafers and thieves on the Wellington waterfront." The policeman says: "Thieves, eh? What are their names, sir?" "Names? Everybody knows their names. The Kaiwharawhara Murderer and the Smiling Seagull."

The policeman would be getting a bit confused!

Wait till I tell you. He takes the Murderer and the Seagull to the police station. "Can't you take the word of the Chief Timekeeper?" says the Murderer to the copper, "we know him well." "What's his name then," the copper asks. "His name? Everybody knows him. He's Terrible Ted, the Tyrant Timekeeper, the greatest standover man on the Wellington waterfront." At the police station the Murderer says to the constable: "Take me to the Senior Sergeant, I know him." The constable says: "Wait until I tell the Senior Sergeant that you two claim you are wharf labourers—but you have no tickets. You say you can vouch for each other—but you don't know each other's names. One of you claims the other is a Murderer! And the Chief Timekeeper says you are both thieves." The Kaiwharawhara Murderer interrupts him: "The Senior Sergeant will vouch for us. We know him." "Well, what's his name?" the constable asks. "*His* name? Everybody knows him, he's the Westport Bruiser," says the Seagull. Anyway, they eventually get into the Senior Sergeant's office. "Excuse me, sir," the constable says, "these two men claim they are wharf labourers, but they have no tickets . . ." The Senior Sergeant laughs. "Ah, they're all right." "Do you know them, sergeant?" the constable asks. "Yes, everybody knows them." "Well, perhaps you at least can tell me their names." The Senior Sergeant says: "Of course I can: that's the Kaiwharawhara Murderer and that's the Smiling Seagull."

Nobody knew anybody's name, eh?

That's why everybody has a nickname on the Wellington waterfront.

22

I'm a Real Crusader Against Acid Stomach

(as told by Billy Borker in the
Pacific Hotel, Manly)

HELLO, Billy, how are things?

Never had it so good, Jerome. Picked the TAB double on Saturday. Better have a drink on the strength of it. Beer?

Think I'll have a whisky instead. The doctor's put me off beer.

Why?

I've got what he calls extreme stomach acidity.

A burning pain rising up from your stomach to your throat? Yes? Well, now, if there's one thing I like above another it's a man with an acid stomach. All me best mates have acid stomachs.

You don't tell.

It's a positive fact. It's the national Australian sickness. But take no notice of doctors. Drink all the beer you want. I'm a real crusader against acid stomach, got a dead-set cure for it: Quick-Eze. Here, just put one of these on your tongue. There, don't chew it up. Two beers for two gentlemen with acid stomachs. Just leave it on your tongue, mate. Did I ever tell you about the time I ran out of Quick-Eze in London?

No, I don't think you did. Hey, this stuff works. The burning pain is going away.

A'course it is. Here's your beer. I've treated a lot of cases with Quick-Eze. Always keep a packet in me pocket. And a carton in the house, since I nearly burned to death in London with acid stomach and no Quick-Eze.

I'll just slip this Quick-Eze tablet into my pocket. Here's luck.

Buy yourself a carton on your way home. The bloke at my corner store nearly collapsed at my feet when I ordered a carton first time. I was going to England on a run job. . . .

Run job?

Yeh, I was at sea in those days and when a new ship was built in England for use in Australia's coastal trade an Australian crew was flown over to the Old Dart to bring her back. Well, I had the luck of the draw and decided to lay in a carton of Quick-Eze to see me out the journey. "A carton? Are you going to open a shop in opposition?" the man at the corner store says when I asked him. "No," I tells him, "I'm going to England. Be away a couple of months. Must have a good supply of Quick-Eze. Can't live without Quick-Eze. I suffer from extreme stomach acidity."

That's what I've got.

Nine Australians out of ten above the age of fifteen have it, mate. Anyway, the corner-store man says to me: "You drink too much beer, that's your trouble. Think you had the only bad stomach in Sydney?" I sort of took a liking to him. My favourite subject is an acid stomach—even if it's someone else's stomach. "Do you suffer from excess acidity?" I asks him. And he says: "I don't know what I suffer from. All I know is I got a stomach like a blast furnace. I've had six X-rays, five different doctors' prescriptions, six bottles of patent medicines, nine tins of stomach powder, and thirteen brands of stomach tablets. I've had rubber tubes dangled down my throat and I've been to four Macquarie Street specialists. I've tried every diet known to man, including a milk diet and a hay diet."

He must have had a terrible stomach.

Did he ever? I says to him, with my best bedside manner: "And what are your symptoms, dear chap?" "It's the pain," he says, "it's terrible. Can't sleep with it. . . ." I'd heard it all before: "It starts in your stomach and rises into your chest and throat? And it burns?" "Burns!" he says. "You can say that again. Sometimes I feel like sending for the fire brigade." I had to be firm with him: "Do you mean to tell me that you have put up with extreme acidity while you have whole cartons of Quick-Eze on your shelves?" Anyway, I pulled a packet out of the carton and broke off a tablet. "Here, open your mouth," I says. "Don't chew it, just leave it on your tongue, and go and serve your customers."

Did it work?

A'course it worked. He stopped by the cash register, suspended in mid-air. "It's gone," he says, "the burning pain has gone!" "Think nothing of it," I says, "you won't have to send for the fire brigade and you'll be able to buy your Quick-Eze wholesale." I got carried away and quoted from old Omar: "I wonder often what the vintners buy one half so precious as the stuff they sell." "What did you say?" he asks. "Just a quotation from Omar Khayyam." "Omar K.M. *who*?" he asks. "Skip it," I says.

Omar K.M. who? You're rambling again. Thought you said you were going to tell me . . .

How I ran out of Quick-Eze in London. That's what I am telling you. My father wouldn't have worn you for a bet. Have another beer, and I'll tell you. I feel in a generous mood today. Well, I get on the plane and the old acid is working overtime in my comic cuts on account I'm nervous about aeroplanes; even Quick-Eze can't cure an aeroplane crash from twenty thousand feet. I suck a tablet for a while to kill the acid so I can get on the beer. There's a bloke next to me with long hair and a beard, a scientist. "Have a drink," I says. "Not me," he says, "the doctors have put me on the water wagon. I suffer from heart burn, flatulence. . . ." I gave him a Quick-Eze tablet. Needless to say, he got quick relief. I gave him two packets and advised him to write to Australia for regular supplies. That man could split the atom, no doubt, but it took Quick-Eze to split the acid in his stomach. Well, on the way to London I cured an air hostess of indigestion, two seamen of heartburn, a steward of ulcers, and the pilot of flatulence. And I gave each of them a couple of packets out of the carton in my airways bag.

The plot thickens.

Yeh, Big-hearted Borker, they call me. Can't resist giving Quick-Eze to people with acid stomachs. In London we had to wait for the ship. In four days I cured a Thames docker, a girl from a Soho clip joint, a cockney barman, and Rolf Harris of acid stomach with well-chosen doses of Quick-Eze. And I cured the head waiter at the pub I was staying at. News got around and people used to call at the pub seeking treatment for indigestion. Needless to say, I treated them all without fear or favour. Then suddenly, I realised I had only one packet left. And do you know what happened?

I can hardly wait.

I began to hoard the Quick-Eze like a miser—but I get down to two and a half tablets, and still no sign of the ship sailing. Soon I was down to one tablet. So I went on the National Health. The doctor examines me and says: "You're about as fit as a man who drinks too much beer can expect to be." "I know that," I says, "but I get this burning pain." The doctor pulls his stethoscope out of his ears. "Burning pain," he says, "a burning pain that rises from your stomach up your chest to your throat?" "That and no other," I says. "Well, there's no cure for that. It's chronic stomach acidity. I've had it for ten years and I've got it right now." Well this was a great moment for me. I'd been known to treat as many as four cases of acidity a day, but they were ordinary Australian mortals. This was an English doctor.

And you gave him your last tablet?

"Open your mouth," I says. And my last Quick-Eze tablet relieved his pain in ten seconds flat. "Where can I get those tablets," he asks. "If you pay for a cablegram, I'll get a carton over by express air mail," I says. I cabled my corner-store man. But did I suffer while I was waiting! I went from sweet shop to chemist shop asking for Quick-Eze. And do you know what? They'd never even heard of it. No wonder the country's going to the dogs. I bought different powders, tablets, and mixtures until I was frothing at the mouth but no use.

Then one of my shipmates suggested I go down to the Earl's Court Road and find some Australians. I went there and started pulling people up in the street. In six hours I only struck one Australian and he didn't have acid stomach for some reason. He suggested I try Australia House. I'd find Australians there and most Australians are civilised people—with acid stomachs. I took a cab, me chest was burning like a hot water pipe. I says to the sheila at the desk: "Have you got any Quick-Eze?" She looks down her nose and says, "No" with an Oxford accent. Then I saw a fellow leaning lazily against the wall, hat on the back of his head, a home-made fag dangling from a corner of his mouth, reading the racing page of a newspaper. "You wouldn't happen to have any Quick-Eze, mate, would you?" I pleaded. "I would, mate, and that's for sure," he says.

So he gave you some Quick-Eze.

And put out the fire. Gave me a packet and it lasted me until the carton arrived by air the day before the ship sailed. On the way home I treated two firemen, the bosun, and the second mate.

A fair yarn but not up to your usual standard.

That's not a yarn; it's a story of a national affliction —acid stomach. I got to be going. Hurroo.

What's your hurry?

Got to catch the shops before they close. I'm nearly out of Quick-Eze.

Think I'll join you. You've made another convert. It's like I say: I'm a real crusader against acid stomach.

124

23

How the Ragged Duke Bagged the Ashes

(as told by Billy Borker in the
Sylvania Hotel, Sylvania)

GOODDAY, Billy.

You know, Jerome, with a name like yours you ought to get a nickname. Australian seamen all have nicknames. Knew a bloke one time—sailed out of Newcastle—they called him the Ragged Duke.

Strange name, that—the Ragged Duke.

Nothing strange about it. Aboard ship he had no clothes, used to borrow working gear from a fireman on another watch. Shabby as a Queensland tramp.

Why call such a man a duke?

Coming to that. Ashore he had clothes in pawnshops in every port. Tweed coats, evening suits, boxer hats, spats. The best dressed man on the coast.

The Ragged Duke. Australian irony.

Did I ever tell you about the time he bagged the ashes?

No, I don't think you did. Have a beer and tell me about it.

I'll force one down just to be sociable.

Bag the Ashes? Another cricket story?

No, about bagging ashes from the fires of a coal burner. A'course, all the ships are oil burners now, or new fangled motor ships. Firemen are a dying race. Only one man where there used to be four. It's a funny thing. On the old coal burners we worked like horses, sweating with coal dust in our throats, yet some firemen complained when the coal burners went off the coast. When they tell you about the good old days, mate, don't believe a word of it.

You were a fireman on the coal burners were you?

That's for sure. I knew the Ragged Duke well. I was on the ship with him, the time he bagged the ashes.

Tell me about it.

Well, it's a job for four men to pull the fires and bag the ashes. But the Ragged Duke done it on his own, this particular time I'm telling you about.

How did he come to do it, that's what I'm trying to get at?

It happened this way. The old Ragged was a good bloke, a good worker and a good unionist, but he was fond of the gargle, see. He'd break out now and then and when he did, you couldn't get him out of the cart to turn to.

Cart?

Bed. We were going from Newcastle to Whyalla in the old *Iron River* and the Ragged Duke got on the plonk. Threw a deucer every watch for three days.

Deucer?

Someone else had to do a double, do his watch. Well, there's talk about it on the ship and the delegates call a meeting, see, and the crew delivers the Ragged Duke an ultimatum; unless he turns to and does his work they're going to report him to the union.

I don't blame them.

Every man has his weakness, mate. Anyway, the

126

Ragged Duke pulls himself together. He's feeling crook, but he starts doing his watches again.

How did he come to—what was it?—bag the ashes?

Never get ahead of your story, my father always said. Anyway, in Whyalla, what should be astern of the *Iron River*, but her sister ship, the *Iron Mountain*. You couldn't tell those ships apart, mate, the dead spitting replica of each other.

What's that got to do with it?

Got a lot to do with it. The old Ragged knew some of the boys on the *Iron Mountain*, see, so he goes aboard to a party on the Saturday night. Gets full, needless to say, and flakes out in someone else's bed. But he remembers he has to turn to in the morning in the ash gang. So he manages to set an alarm clock for eight. Forgets it's Sunday morning when the ash gang doesn't turn to until nine o'clock. Well, he wakes up next morning with the mother and father of a hangover but he struggles out when the alarm goes off, borrows someone else's working gear from the change room, and goes below. He gets the long rake and pulls the first fire, a sweat rag tied around his face. He hoses down the great heap of red-hot coal until the stokehold's an inferno of sizzling smoke. He begins to wonder where the others are. He's got a guilty conscience about throwing deucers, so he's sort of pleased to be working when the others are late. So he pulls the second fire, waters her down, and still no sign of his watch mates. So he starts shovelling the ashes into the bags, working like a contract miner on Christmas Eve, sweating, aching, tired out. It usually took four big firemen two hours on job and finish to pull the fires and bag the ashes— and the old Ragged Duke did the whole job on his own in one hour flat, a world record they say in the water-front pubs.

Fair enough, but that story's not up to your usual standard. No twist at the end.

Well, the old Ragged fills the last bag and sits down exhausted, too tired to go up the fiddley for a quick gulp of the grape, when in comes the second engineer, name of Suttley, friendly as a bag full of Queensland taipans. "Where's your mates?" he asked the Ragged Duke. The old Ragged was a staunch man. "They were here a minute ago," he says. "They'll be back in a minute, no doubt." The engineer eyes the old Ragged suspicious-like. "What's your name?" he asks. "You know me, Second, the Ragged Duke from Newcastle." "And what ship is this?" the engineer asks. "Fair go, Second, think I don't know what ship I'm on? The *Iron River*, a'course." "This happens to be the *Iron Mountain*," the engineer tells him.

So that's the twist.

You wouldn't want to know. The Ragged Duke had pulled the fires and bagged the ashes—on the wrong ship.

Quite a character. What became of him?

He gave the grog away after that. Last I heard of him he'd formed a group of Alcoholics Anonymous on the old S.S. *Ellaroo*.

24

How Honest Hambone Tricked the Waterfront D's

(as told by Billy Borker in the
Brighton Hotel, Brighton Beach)

FUNNY, all right.

What's so funny?

The nickname of the seaman you told me about
—the Ragged Duke.

Funnier nicknames than that on the Sydney waterfront. One bloke there they called London Fog.

What was the purpose of that?

He wouldn't lift, mate—he wouldn't lift. Another
bloke they called Honest Hambone.

How would a man get a name like that?

There's always a reason behind a nickname. This
fella was a bit of a raffle king, like myself. One Christmas week he raffled a ham. Every time he and his mate
got hungry they cut a few slices off it. By the time
the raffle was drawn on Christmas Eve only the bone
was left. They called him Honest Hambone after that.

Must have been a character.

Was he ever. A bit of a tealeaf, but . . .

Tealeaf?

Thief.

Be a lot of thieves on the waterfront, I suppose?

No more than on the Stock Exchange, mate, as I've told you before. Anyway, nobody ever caught old Honest Hambone stealing anything. The waterfront D's were always searching his gladstone bag, but they never caught him. Fair sent them up the wall, it did.

Be an annoying thing that.

Wouldn't it ever. The D's used to lie awake at night thinking up ways to catch him. One time there was a shipment of chiming clocks came in from Switzerland. The lollipops reckoned the old Hambone couldn't be able to resist such a charming gift. So they went down the hold in the middle of the night and set all the chiming clocks to go off at five o'clock—Brahms' Lullaby. At five o'clock you'd think there was a symphony orchestra playing as the wharfies came off the day shift. You could hear Brahms' Lullaby a mile away. So the D's grab Honest Hambone and search his bag but it was empty. "I don't go for that classical music," he told them. "I'm a Beatle fan." While they were searching Hambone about a dozen wharfies went through the gate to the accompaniment of Brahms' Lullaby.

You said that Honest Hambone tricked them. . . .

So he did. I was working on the Sydney waterfront at the time, so I ought to know.

You know, Mister Borker—I mean, Billy, I've worked it out that, judging by all the things you've done you must be more than a hundred years old.

Have you now, young Jerome? Well, one night the waterfront D's are standing at the gate chewing the rag about not being able to catch Honest Hambone when he choofs along wheeling a barrow full of straw. The coppers rub their hands with glee. Got him at last.

They search through the straw and under it. But the wheelbarrow was empty. Next night, up choofs old Honest Hambone again wheeling his barrow full of straw. They search it again, but it's empty. They're suspicious, see, so they have a conference with the customs officials and they decide to examine the wheelbarrow. They turn it over. Pull the bottom of it to see if it was false, but found nothing. Honest Hambone's feelings were hurt: "You've ruined me barrow," he says, "you'll have to put it together again." Well, they put the bottom back on the barrow; and Honest Hambone puts the straw back in it and away he goes.

Did they ever catch him?

Next night, sure enough, along comes Honest Hambone still wheeling his barrow. But a customs official had worked out an idea. They searched the straw and found nothing. So with that they took the wheel off the barrow.

Oh, something hidden in the spokes?

That's what they must have thought; but they found nothing. They went over that barrow with a fine tooth comb, even poked a stick down the hollow of the handle bars. But the cupboard was bare, as the saying goes. They were going around the bend by this time. "You'll have to repair my barrow," Honest Hambone said, "or I'll sue the Government." Well, they put the barrow together as best they could. Anyway, sharp at five next afternoon regular as the clock along comes Hambone wheeling his wheelbarrow. By force of habit they searched the straw, but found nothing, needless to say. So one of the detectives says to Honest H.: "Listen, we know you're the biggest thief on the waterfront. If we promise not to book you will you tell

". . . They searched the straw and found nothing!"

us what you're stealing?" Now, Hambone had been brought up never to trust a policeman so he says to one of the customs officials: "If I tell you, you'll promise not to book me?" "Cross me heart and hope to die," the customs man says pleading. "Just tell us, please tell us—what are you stealing?" "Wheelbarrows," Honest Hambone told them, "there's a shipment of wheelbarrows being unloaded at Number Seven North Wharf."

Not bad, not bad. Gee, look at the time, I must be going.

Hooroo. If you know of anyone who wants to buy a good wheelbarrow, I know where you can get one cheap.

25

The Greatest Compo Doctor in the Southern Hemisphere

(as told by Billy Borker in the
Steyne Hotel, Manly)

You don't look too good today, Billy.

Sick as a swagman's dog. On compo.

What's the trouble?

Crook back.

That's an old Workers' Compensation trick. Have a drink.

Now, just a minute, mate, what hope would a working man have without a bit of honest compo? As a matter of fact, my back is real crook but the doctor didn't believe me, either. "Bend down and pick up that piece of paper," he says. I bent down and couldn't get up again. And he says: "You're the greatest actor since John Barrymore." It's always the same; when you're telling the truth no one believes you—especially compo doctors.

Compensation doctors obey the ethics of the profession.

I've struck a few that could have fooled me. A compo doctor's job is to save the insurance companies money by passing you fit for work.

You have the right to consult your own doctor.

You're a natural born defender of the Establishment, mate. But I'll admit things have improved lately. In the old days, a compo doctor would send a blind man back to work driving a truck.

I don't believe it.

Positive fact. I knew a compo doctor who sent a miner back to work with a broken neck after an explosion in the Kurri Kurri mine. After that, sick miners used to walk fifty miles to Newcastle to avoid him.

Do you mean to say you've never met a good compensation doctor?

Well, come to think of it, I have. When I was at sea I struck the greatest compo doctor in the Southern Hemisphere. A shipping company's doctor, he was. Name of Hawkins, at Newcastle. He gave me a fortnight one time for a sore throat I got singing "The Wild Colonial Boy" at a Union Social.

You don't tell.

Positive fact. His dead-set minimum was a fortnight, whether there was anything wrong with you or not.

How did he get that way?

Well, there was various theories. Some said he had once sent a seaman back to work with a bad appendix which burst off Nobby's Head lighthouse and he died. Anyway, after that Doctor Hawkins put 'em all on compo—regardless.

Must have been popular with the company.

You can say that again. As popular as a poker machine at a parsons' picnic. Was popular with steel workers, seamen and wharfies but . . .

I'll bet he was.

Yeh, he gave out compo without fear or favour. It used to be funny at the clinic. Six doctors there. All the compo cases outside Doctor Hawkins' door. Expectant women and old pensioners with colds or malnutrition went to the other doctors; but all the compo cases waited in a long queue for Doctor Hawkins.

Hardly fair to the company, old chap.

Well, it done away with abuses of the Workers' Compensation Act. No more sick workers being sent back to work. No more workers playing compo tricks: no one in Newcastle bothered using the old scrubbing brush to create rashes or clamping a tobacco tin over the skin to get a nice neat compo cut. Doctor Hawkins should have been knighted, a lot of people reckoned. The most popular man in the district. Yet some people were crook on him—especially captains of coastal ships sailing out of Newcastle.

Why was that?

Well, every time a ship came into Newcastle, some of the crew would pay off on compo. Then the Second Mate and the Engineer would have to hang around the seamen's pick-up every day waiting for a full crew.

An annoying thing that.

There was one skipper on the old freighter *Iron River*; Mad Mick Burton they called him. Swore he'd get rid of Doctor Hawkins if it was the last thing he did. Mad Mick had never been sick in his life and reckoned everyone else should be the same. I'll get rid of that Hawkins some day and save the company a fortune, he used to tell the Second Mate.

Don't blame him.

Anyway, to make a long story short, the old *Iron River* sailed into Newcastle just before Christmas—and half the crew made a call on Doctor Hawkins and paid off on compo. Mad Mick Burton hit the roof. The Mate and the Engineer went to the pick-up every day but there was no labour available on account of the festive season. Mad Mick had had enough. He called a meeting of the officers midships and he says: "I'm going to put a stop to this Hawkins once and for all. I'm going up to the clinic to see him. I'll tell him a thing or two."

And how did he get on?

Well, Mad Mick choofs off up to the clinic to see Doctor Hawkins. The officers wait for him. The First Mate says: "Captain Burton will put a stop to this crazy compo and get the ships turning around again." The Chief Engineer says: "I hope he doesn't do anything violent." Hours go by and they wait at the top of the gangway. At last they see Mad Mick coming along the wharf. As he comes up the gangway, the First Mate says: "Well, Skipper, did you see Doctor Hawkins?" "I saw him all right," the Skipper says. "Did you tell him off?" "I'm a sick man," the Captain replied. "A chill on the kidneys. Doctor Hawkins paid me off on a month's compo."

And what became of Doctor Hawkins?

All good things must come to an end. He died eventually. Had the biggest funeral ever held in Newcastle. The greatest compo doctor in the Southern Hemisphere.

26

The Hunger for Knowledge is a Powerful Thing

(as told by Billy Borker in the
Earl of Zetland Hotel, Adelaide)

WHAT's the book?
A Modern Prospector's Guide. How to find
gold in ten easy lessons.

Do you read much?

A fair bit. Not as much as I did before television was
invented, but . . .

Books are a wonderful thing.

Must be a funny game, writing. A writer writes a
book—on his own. And a reader reads it—on his own.
No audience like a musician or an actor—or a yarn-
spinner.

Think of the knowledge spread by books through
the ages.

Yes, I've learned a lot from books—but I don't go
for those made-up stories about murderers, thieves, businessmen. . . .

You told me that before. Why are you reading about
prospecting?

I've done a bit of prospecting in me time. Like to
keep up to date. Matter of fact, I was out prospecting

when I learned the real power of the hunger for knowledge.

Have a drink and tell me about it.

I'll force one down—just to be sociable. Before the war it was. Me and Timetable Tommy went prospecting north of Kalgoorlie. In the desert, a hundred miles from the nearest railhead. Well, we worked like slaves to sink a deep shaft. Thought we were on a quartz reef, but struck solid rock. Timetable got jack of it, after that, so when the truck came out with mail and the weekly supplies of grub and water, he took a lift back and left me there. Well, I started to sink another shaft. Slow work on your own; and very lonely, especially at night. Used to lie awake listening to the dingoes howling and wishing I'd shot through with me mate. Then, one night, I saw a light in the distance. Seemed to be fairly close by, so I headed towards it. I must have walked three or four miles: a single light always seems closer than it really is in the bush at night. There was a crescent moon casting weird shadows. . . .

I don't see what this has to do with the hunger for knowledge.

Wait till I tell you. You know what my father always said. . . . Anyway, eventually I get near this light, see. And it turns out to be a carbide lamp in a lean-to.

Lean-to?

A poor man's tent. Like an aboriginal's miamia. This one was made of logs and bark. When I get near it, I can see an old codger sitting on a small box beside a big box with the lamp on it. He's shuffling a pack of cards. So I thinks, a poker school. The mateship of a game of cards was just what I needed. I'm just going to speak, when the old fella deals himself about twelve cards. He fans them out in his hand, looks at them, then turns them face down on the table. Then he screws up his face and reels off the cards in a high-pitched cackling voice. "Ten of hearts, jack of diamonds, seven of clubs, ace of spades, six of hearts. . . ." I go a bit closer and you should have seen him. Long white hair, moustache and beard. Eyes sticking out like you could knock them off with a stick. Bony hands like skeleton's covered with withered yellow leather. Bare, dirty feet. Holes in the knees of his old dungarees and a flannel singlet gone hard with sweat and dust. He deals himself another hand, turns the cards down on the table. And he reels off the cards again. "Ace of clubs, four of hearts, seven of diamonds, jack of spades, ten of clubs. . . ." I thinks, what have I struck here? He's there on his Pat Malone, see, talking to himself, silly as a two-bob watch. I decides to make meself scarce and get back to camp.

What was he doing?

That's what I was wondering. As Bernard Shaw once said: "You ain't heard nothing yet." He's got an old clock there. So he winds it up and puts it on the box. Then he steps back to the entrance and listens with his hand cupped around his ear. And he backs away from the clock towards me, with his hand to his ear, listening. Before I could get away, he bumps into me, see, and swings around. One of those mad hermits who hang around old goldfields until they die. He put the wind up me, I can tell you.

I'll bet he did.

"What's your name?" he asks me, as if it was natural for someone to stumble into his camp in the middle of the night. "Billy Borker," I says, backing away.

He repeats the name: "Billy Borker", then dashes into the hut, grabs the lamp, and holds it in front of my face. "Billy Borker," he says. "Eyes blue. Complexion dark. Height five foot eleven. I'll remember you if we meet again."

Must have been a strange experience?

Yes it was.

What was the purpose of him repeating the denomination of the cards, listening to the clock, and committing your name and description to memory?

Well, it turned out that he'd seen an advertisement in an old newspaper that had come out to his camp wrapped around some groceries. He cut out the coupon and took one of them courses in Pelmanism that used to be advertised. You know: "Train the mind, memory, and personality. Strengthen your will. Improve your memory and hearing. Increase your powers of concentration." I couldn't help thinking: what use would such a course be to him? There he was, a hundred miles from the railway, a hundred and fifty miles from the nearest human habitation, seventy-five years old, and as mad as a hatter. What would he want with a course in Pelmanism?

Yes, it shows the power of the hunger for knowledge all right.

Either that or the power of modern advertising. I've never been able to decide which.

27

Joe Parsnip Stumbled into a Jeweller's Shop

(as told by Billy Borker in the
Savoy Plaza Hotel, Perth)

STILL got your nose in that book about prospecting,
I see?

Yeh, a good book, as a matter of fact. Knows
what he's talking about, this fella.

Did you do any good prospecting, yourself?

No, never ever struck it rich. Got pay dirt at times.
But me and Timetable Tommy were unlucky north
of Kalgoorlie. Old Joe Parsnip stumbled into a
jeweller's shop not far from where our shaft had been.

A jeweller's shop? Have a drink and tell me about it.

Thanks. A jeweller's shop is what they call a mineral
formation in rock. Minerals form in a bugh—B-U-G-H
—a hole in the rock; looks beautiful, glistens like a
jeweller's shop. And that mineral can be pure gold.

This Joe Parsnip was a gold prospector?

No, he was a night-soil carter, in Kalgoorlie. Wouldn't
have known a nugget of gold from a clinker of coal.
But he had an Irish mate, name of Sandy Panter, who
could smell gold-bearing land a mile off. Sandy sunk
a shaft near a quartz reef north of Kalgoorlie. But Joe
Parsnip was a know-all: "We should dig a hole over
there," he says, pointing to rocky ground to the west.

"That's solid rock," Sandy tells him scornfully, "and you don't dig a hole, you sink a shaft."

Don't say you're going to tell me he struck gold in solid rock.

This story was told to me by Gold-dust Riddell in a pub in Kalgoorlie. He knew old Joe Parsnip well. I'm just repeating the story the way he told it to me and he was the most truthful gold prospector who ever sunk a shaft. Joe Parsnip actually found the gold *before* the war. I went back *after* the war, and that's when Gold-dust Riddell told me the story. While Sandy Panter drove a shaft into the reef, Joe Parsnip blasted a shaft into the rock. And he stumbled into a jeweller's shop—with a great nugget of pure gold. Joe called Sandy over and Sandy fainted on the spot. That's how Joe knew it was gold. So they put the nugget into the back of their old car and drove into Kalgoorlie. The biggest find since the Welcome Stranger, worth fifty-five thousand quid—in the days before the value was taken out of the pound.

Gold is where you find it, eh?

A very true saying. But gold affects different men in different ways. It had a funny effect on old Joe Parsnip. He was a tall lean man of doubtful age. Been poor all his life. Walked with his feet at a quarter-past nine. Staggers into the pub and dumps the great nugget on the counter. "Fill 'em up," he yells, "the drinks are on Joe Parsnip." Well everyone gathers around the nugget. The pub stayed open all night with Joe buying the drinks and little Sandy trying to remind him that half the nugget was his. Next day they go down to the Government Assayer's Office, get the gold valued and deposit the money in the bank. Well, it's the talk of the town. Old Joe Parsnip gave up his night-soil round and went on the spree. Some diggers turn mean when they strike it rich, but Joe was the opposite. He bought a new American truck. One day he staggers out of the pub and hands the keys to an old drunk sitting on the edge of the horse trough. "See that truck there? Well, it's yours, mate," he says. "I got no use for a truck," the drunk says. Old Joe turned nasty: "When Joe Parsnip gives you a present, you take it, see?"

A fool and his money are soon parted.

Well, pretty soon a mob of hangers-on are following Joe Parsnip wherever he goes, and him boasting about how he knows all about prospecting. He forgets his mate has gone home to Mother Ireland with his share, and without him Joe wouldn't know a quartz reef from a seam of coal. Anyway, Joe takes a fancy to a barmaid named Maggie, see. And, a'course, she takes a fancy to old Joe's bank account. So, when he suggests they get engaged, she agrees. "What would you like for an engagement present?" Joe asks her. "What about buying me a pub," she says for a joke. Joe bought her the pub on the spot.

Did they settle down together in the pub?

No, Gold-dust Riddell reckoned that Joe Parsnip spent the next ten years trying to get it back off her.

Go broke, did he?

Kept telling everyone he knew where there was another jeweller's shop, north of where the railway line cut out. So, one day, he goes down to the rail-way station and tells the stationmaster he wants to buy a train to go prospecting it. "You can't *buy* a train," the stationmaster says, "but you can hire a special." Joe closes the deal and fills the train with all sorts of mining equipment, beer, wine, food, champagne and a hundred free-loading passengers. Everyone gets drunk including the driver, fireman and guard. You could hear them singing a mile away, Gold-dust Riddell reckoned.

Did they get any gold?

No, it was only beginner's luck, Joe stumbling on that jeweller's shop in the first place. When the grog ran out, the train brought them all back to Kalgoorlie. Old Joe Parsnip was broke in less than a month and the hangers-on left him for dead.

And what became of him? Did he go back to the night-soil carting?

That's what I asked Gold-dust Riddell. Gold had got into Joe's blood, mate. He fossicked around for ten years, but did no good. And, it was funny, I can remember as if it was yesterday: Gold-dust Riddell had just told us the story, when we hear a loud voice at the other end of the bar: "Fill 'em up. The drinks are on Joe Parsnip", and there he was, white-haired but as large as life, thumping another great nugget of gold on the counter.

I hope he looked after his money the second time.

Well, I don't rightly know, I left Kalgoorlie a few days later. But when I was waiting at the railway station I saw old Joe Parsnip, a barmaid on his arm, and surrounded by a mob of hangers-on, hiring a train to go prospecting in.

28

"How Would I Be"

(as told by Billy Borker in the
William Hotel, Sydney)

Y OU'VE certainly got a fund of good stories. Where
did you get them all?

I told you; from me father.

He must have had a vivid imagination.

Imagination? They're all true! I don't like these made-up stories you read in books and see on television. . . .

So you've said before. What would be the best Australian story you ever heard?

Well, I reckon the most fair dinkum Australian story ever told was about the World's Worst Whinger.

The World's Worst Worrier. You've told me that one.

Not the World's Worst Worrier. The World's Worst Whinger. A different story altogether. I call it: "How would I be?"

Have another drink and tell me about it.

I don't mind if I do. I first met this bloke—the World's Worst Whinger—in a shearing shed in Queensland during the Depression. I asked him an innocent question: "How would you be?" Well, he dropped the sheep he was shearing, spat, and fixed me with a pair of bitter eyes and he says: "How would I be? How would you expect me to be? Get a load of me, will you? Dags on every inch of me hide; drinking me own sweat; swallowing dirt with every breath I breathe; shearing sheep that should have been dogs' meat years ago; working for the lousiest boss in Australia; frightened to leave because the old woman's looking for me in Brisbane with a maintenance order. How would I be? I haven't tasted beer for weeks and the last glass I had was knocked over by some clumsy coot before I finished it."

He must have been a whinger, all right.

The world's worst, like I told you. Next time I met him he was in an army camp in Melbourne. He'd joined the A.I.F. "How would you be?" I asked him. "How would I be? Get a load of this outfit. Look at me flamin' hat. Size nine and a half and I take six and a half. Get an eyeful of these strides—you could hide a blasted brewery horse in the seat of them and still have room for me. And get on to these boots, will yer? There's enough leather in 'em to make a full set of harness. And some idiot brass-hat told me this was a man's outfit. How would I be? How would you *expect* me to be?"

Is this story true?

True? Well most of my stories are true but this one, you might say it's truer than true. I met him next in Tobruk. He was sitting on a box, tin hat over one eye, cigarette butt dangling from his bottom lip, rifle leaning on one knee, cleaning his finger nails with his bayonet. I should have known better but I asked him: "How would you be, Dig?" He swallowed his cigarette butt and stared at me with a malevolent eye. "How would I be? How would I be? How would you expect me to be? Shot at by every Fritz in Africa; eating sand with every meal; flies in me eyes; frightened to go to sleep; expecting to die in this God-forsaken place. And you ask me *how would I be?*"

Did you ever meet him again?

No, he was killed in Tobruk, as a matter of fact.

Well, one thing, he wouldn't do any more whingeing, poor devil.

You know, I dreamt about him the other night.

Yeh?

Yeh. I dreamt I died and went to Heaven. It was as clear as on a television screen. I saw him there in my dream and I asked: "How would you be?" He eyed me with an angelic expression and he says; "How would I be? Get an eyeful of this night-gown, will yer? A man trips over it fifty times a day and takes ten minutes to lift it to scratch his knee. And take a gander at me right wing, feathers falling out of it, a man must be moulting. Cast your eyes over this halo; only me big ears keep the rotten thing on me skull. And just take a Captain Cook at this harp, five strings missing and there's band practice in five minutes. *How would I be? you ask. How would you expect a man to bloody well be?*"

A good story. Yes, a beauty.

The most fair dinkum Australian story ever told. . . .

Author's Note

The Yarns of Billy Borker began, not as the television series that became so well-known in 1964, but as an attempt, as early as twenty years before, to capture on paper Australian folk-narrative yarns. The first one was published in the *Australasian Post* in 1946 when George Johnson was editor. It was called "The Violinist from Chinkapook".

My idea was to make written stories out of material one would normally tell as a yarn in a pub. To achieve this, I found it necessary to leave out narrative, to let a yarn-spinner "tell" the story to a gullible listener. There is a difference between a story and a yarn, too subtle to explain, but over the years, when I got an idea, I instinctively knew when it was a Billy Borker yarn or a literary short story with narrative.

A few Billy Borker stories found their way into print in *Overland*, the *Realist*, the *Territorian*, the *Butchers' Union Journal* and Bill Wannan's *Treasuries*. Nobody took much notice of them.

Borker got his big break when the ABC Programme Department decided to put him on television. It happened this way. The ABC are embarrassed by "holes" lasting five or ten minutes, thanks to their laudable policy of refusing advertisements: when they buy a programme from a commercial TV network overseas, they end up with time originally devoted to the real and imagined qualities of sponsors' products. They

use this time, or some of it, to show swans float-
ing on lakes, ten shilling notes blowing in the wind
and Noeline Pritchard nattering sweet nothings about
Britain. I thought some of the time would be better
devoted to Billy Borker.

I have often been asked where the stories came from.
Billy Borker's answer to that is, of course, that they
are really his father's stories. In my own case, that's
part of the answer, too, for the first and best Australian
yarn-spinner I ever heard was my father Tom Hardy.
"The Greatest Slanter" and "The Violinist from
Chinkapook" are his stories.

The majority of the stories—about seamen, wharfies,
taxi drivers, racecourse tipsters, bagmen, men with acid
stomachs, and compo doctors—arose from my own
experience or the experience of men I drank with in
pubs up and down the coast.

Some of the stories were told to me as fact: the raffle
stories, the one about the old hatter studying Pelmanism
in the desert, about Sam Loxton being trapped at square
leg, and Joe Parsnip stumbling on a "jeweller's shop".

The Melbourne-Sydney argument story is merely a
collection of all the petty arguments ever used, with
the twist at the end based on Stan Moran's Domain
yarn about the difference between Tooth's and Toohey's
beer.

Needing a tall story, I selected the one about the
Northern Territory mosquitoes, and for a shaggy dog
story I settled for the one about the billiard table. I'm
still trying to work up a few typical yarns about the
aborigines—meanwhile, I couldn't resist the one Rolf
Harris told at the Chevron. The legend about the tea-
leafing that went on when the *Aorangi* was being

refitted include the theft and dumping of the grand piano—I like to believe that someone who needed it found that piano outside their back gate.

The New Zealand stories were gathered during a visit to Kiwiland. I am indebted to Ted Coppersmith, a timekeeper on the Wellington waterfront, for the nickname story; and to Harry Dansey, of the *Auckland Star*, for the Maori legends that Te Kore told the Governor-General.

"Not like here in Woolloomooloo" is my version of the Australian's characteristic under-valuation of his own, now fortunately passing away.

The World's Worst Worrier and Pessimist are, like most of the other yarns, worked up to an archetypal level of exaggeration from several bits and pieces of stories. I am working on the themes of the World's Worst Urger and Optimist for a future Borker series.

I gradually learned that I must seek in a yarn something typical that would throw light on the Australian character and myth, the quality of a legend. And I am firmly convinced that, even if the yarns about Honest Hambone, Sheckles Mitchell, Dooley Franks and the Mosquitoes are variants of stories to be heard in other countries, the majority of the yarns of Billy Borker are firmly rooted in the good Australian earth.

What other story could possibly end the television series and the book so aptly as "How would I be?"—the Great Australian whinger? My Borker version follows the one collected by Bill Wannan.

To the Australian yarn-spinner, how the story is told is just as important as the story itself. I have studied their methods from boyhood, and wrote these methods into the stories. And when it came to television, Peter

Carver captured the method and spirit of Borker in a quite remarkable way.

I was brought up in the bush where yarn-spinning is an art, and I was pleased to find the tradition of the folk story still strong in the cities, especially amongst workers and knockabouts. Billy Borker is essentially the yarn-spinner of modern times and cities: he rarely goes back beyond the Depression to the old bush days. His world is the man's world of the pub bar. Women rarely figure in his yarns.

Are any of the stories actually true? Well, as Borker himself puts it, every story is true for the yarn-spinner who tells it. I think something like most of these stories happened in several places, which might explain the variants one strikes; then again the variants might occur as one artistic liar takes over the story from another and uses his own local detail. I cannot actually swear that any one story is true although I've told some of them as fact, more than once. Or, to put it another way: I know most of the stories are true—because I made them up myself.

The story about Sam Loxton seemed to offer a chance to test the truth of a yarn. I sent Sam a copy of the script, seeking his permission to use it on television, and secretly hoping he'd confirm or deny it. Sam replied: "I must admit it makes a very good story—I don't believe you will convince anyone I could bat so long, but good luck with it."

So I'm none the wiser.

According to Vane, whose wonderful drawings add so much to this book, the basis of Australian humour is "you can't win, but you've got to battle." Billy Borker would agree with that.

I've often been asked: who is Billy Borker. Well, he was a mythical character in Victoria during the Depression, a liar and a fearless jumper of rattlers. I never met him. I never saw his name on any electoral role or in any phone book. But my brother gave him substantial existence during the war by putting his name on the manning chart of his unit, and drew his beer and cigarette ration for a time.

If he does exist, he must be about two hundred years old and have followed just about every occupation known in the Great South Land.

He is very real to me, the archetype of the Australian battler, ironic, democratic, suspicious of authority, contemptuous of pomp and privilege. The more they try to keep him down, the better he lives. . . .

He sees something immortal in the ordinary bloke—and probably that's why he tells his yarns, that and because he's an inveterate liar.

HERE'S LUCK

LENNIE LOWER'S wild and uproarious humour has never been surpassed by any other Australian writer. With a truly native sardonic wit and comic imagination he was to our literature what "Mo" was to our stage. HERE'S LUCK was his only novel, and it quickly became, and remained, a best-seller.

Set in Sydney during the early depression years, the novel has for its hero and narrator Mr Gudgeon, who refuses to be dismayed either by financial uncertainty or by — to use his own phrase — the "gimme girls" of the flaming twenties. Mr Gudgeon's wife, Agatha, leaves him as the story opens, the cause of their quarrel being their son, Stanley, an inventive but unreliable young man. Father and son manage to fend for themselves very hilariously in pubs, gambling dens, cafes, race-courses, and in their own increasingly battered home, where they are joined by Agatha Gudgeon's wealthy brother from the bush and, from time to time, by a weird and wonderful assortment of characters of the type who always materialize to enliven that kind of party which Mr Gudgeon invariably intends to be a "quiet, respectable turnout", but which, somehow, never is.

THE SPECIALIST

BY

Chic Sale

**MORE THAN 2,500,000 COPIES SOLD!
NOW PUBLISHED IN 12 COUNTRIES!**

LEM PUTT is THE SPECIALIST — a man who has found his calling. He's the champion privy builder of Sangamon County.

THIS IS HIS STORY.